This book is a must read for everyone trying to influence and change people's lives in a positive way. It's a GREAT business book, but it's also much more than a business book. I plan to get a copy for every Hay House author.

—**Reid Tracy**, CEO, Hay House, Inc.

Even though I am a 30+ year veteran in direct marketing, this book made me realize how much there is still to learn about being an excellent marketer . . . and a human being as well. As one of the heroes among heart-based entrepreneurs on the planet, Jeff has written possibly the most important book about both direct response marketing and entrepreneurship in the last decade.

Anyone who thinks the word "launch" refers only to online marketing hasn't been paying attention to direct response marketing over the last five decades (or more). And anyone who thinks that Jeff Walker hasn't earned the right to own the word "launch" in today's marketing landscape also hasn't been paying attention.

LAUNCH is a must read for anyone in business today—experienced or novice—who needs to get their product or service out to the world . . . and wants to do it with integrity and power.

—**Brian Kurz**, Executive Vice President, Boardroom, Inc.

This is not just a book. It's a license to print money. (Okay, maybe I'm overstating it a bit, but not by much.) I used Jeff's Product Launch Formula to create a seven-figure-plus business I absolutely love. And unlike some successful entrepreneurs, he holds nothing back. It's all here—a proven strategy, real-world examples, and step-by-step instructions—everything you need to create a business you're crazy about while making an incredible living doing it.

—**Michael Hyatt**, *New York Times* Bestselling Author
and Founder of PlatformUniversity.com

The first day of launching a new business has always been a stressful, nerve-racking time. But since applying Jeff Walker's ideas, we've turned these "launch days" into moments of celebration, success, and amazing cash flow as our businesses have managed to pull in incredible customer demand on day one. This has added millions to our bottom line and raised the valuation of our company immensely as day-one sales trumped all expectation.

—**Vishen Lakhiani**, Founder and CEO, Mindvalley

This isn't a book as much as it is a recipe and a blueprint for changing you and your family's financial fortune. It breaks down everything from the Seed Launch, where you start completely from scratch, all the way up to the mega JV Launches that can bring in millions in a matter of days. The process definitely takes some work, but if you get the process down and use it, then you can have nearly instant sales and momentum in your business. Not only will following Jeff's formula make your success more possible, it will make it more probable. So buy Jeff's book—after all, he's the guy who sold a million dollars of his product in a single hour! *LAUNCH* has both of our full endorsements, and it can change your business and your life.

—**Joe Polish** and **Dean Jackson**, ILoveMarketing.com

When it comes to Internet marketing, Jeff Walker is a bonafide genius. Now with *LAUNCH*, he maps out exactly how you can successfully market any product or service online. A must read for all serious entrepreneurs.

—**Randy Gage**, Author of the *New York Times* Bestseller, *Risky Is the New Safe*

This book isn't just for people who want to make a lot of money in their businesses really fast. This is for people who want to live their best life, doing what they were born to do, and serving the world. I highly recommend this book to anyone that wants to make a bigger impact along with a much bigger income.

—**Christian Mickelson**, CEO of CoachesWithClients.com

Wow! What can you say about Jeff Walker? This guy owns the launch space. Believe me—if you're looking to launch a product, business, or even a book, then pick up this book and read it NOW. I guarantee you won't regret it.

—**Eric T. Wagner**, Founder and CEO of Mighty Wise Academy, Writer on Forbes

CMF

Hampshire County Council

WITHDRAWN

SC 4/17

Get **more** out of libraries

Please return or renew this item by the last date shown.

You can renew online at www.hants.gov.uk/library

Or by phoning 0300 555 1387

Hampshire
County Council

C015973168

This is a GREAT book about launching products and growing businesses, but it's about so much more. It's about creating a movement, making an impact, and delivering huge value into the marketplace—and it's based on experience and results. If you want to bring your product, business, or movement into the world in a big way, then *LAUNCH* is your recipe book.

—**Daniel G. Amen**, MD, Author of *Change Your Brain,*
Change Your Life and eight other *New York Times* Bestsellers

The title of this book, *LAUNCH*, is uniquely appropriate because Jeff Walker is the pioneer innovator of online marketing launches, as well as the online marketing industry's foremost teacher. The careers of thousands of successful online entrepreneurs have already been launched by Jeff's extraordinarily practical concepts, structures, strategies, tools, and processes. *LAUNCH* is a must read for all marketers—the go-to handbook for making money selling anything on the Internet.

—**Dan Sullivan**, President and Founder of The Strategic Coach

It took me four years to grow my first business to $5 million. Using Jeff Walker's product launch model, I was able to hit $5 million in sales—in a brand-new business niche—my first year. Jeff has created one of the most important innovations in marketing in the last 100 years.

—**Eben Pagan**, Founder of Hot Topic Media and Serial Online Entrepreneur

Business is a succession of launches—new products, projects, promotions, incentives, partnerships, etc. To succeed you'll need to master the launch. To do so you'll want to study the master of the launch—Jeff Walker. Ten thousand hours and millions of dollars later, he has figured it out. Read this book and shorten your path to profits dramatically.

—**Darren Hardy**, Publisher and Founding Editor
of *SUCCESS* and *New York Times* Bestselling Author of
The Compound Effect—Jumpstart Your Income, Your Life, Your Success

If I could say one word about Jeff Walker and *LAUNCH*, it would be: IMPACT. If you are looking for a huge positive impact on your business, your family, or in life, then *LAUNCH* is a must read. Don't walk to get a copy . . . run, and let Jeff Walker help you create a great legacy for those around you.

—**JB Glossinger**, Founder of MorningCoach.com

In the early days of Web marketing, it was complete freaking chaos online. We knew we had unprecedented access to vast global audiences, but we lacked a simple, elegant way of introducing new products and closing sales.

Enter Jeff Walker . . . who arrived well-versed in old-school direct marketing, coupled with a unique early-adopter's grasp of the potential online. He explained his idea to me, early on, as simply turning a damn good sales letter on its side . . . and using every aspect of this powerful new technology to attract prospects, build their desire to the breaking point, and then transform their lives by fulfilling on the promises that drove them nuts over an extended process of education, sharing, and giving away teasingly good samples.

The launch formula he perfected produced results for us far beyond any of our other online marketing efforts . . . time after time after time. It was stunning. And fun. And elegant in its simplicity. Jeff codified the way online launches will be conducted for generations to come.

—**John Carlton**, Legendary Copywriter and Author of *The Simple Writing System* and *The Entrepreneur's Guide to Getting Your Shit Together*

I've known Jeff Walker for several years—I've watched the way he does business. It's 100% based on building value, and that's exactly what this book does. In *LAUNCH* he gives you the proven recipe for launching your product or business. Jeff teaches from experience, and he teaches with huge heart and great humility. His strategies are both revolutionary and incredibly effective.

—**Janet Bray Attwood**, *New York Times* Bestselling Coauthor of *The Passion Test*

Jeff has a long track record of overdelivering, and *LAUNCH* is no exception. It's packed with real-world case studies, usable step-by-step advice, and the kind of insights you get only from someone who's been there, done that. This is probably the most valuable book you'll read this year.

—**Paul Myers**, Publisher of TalkBizNews.com

I was lucky enough to spend a day in a small room with just a few dozen people listening to Jeff Walker teach his heart out. Every person in the room was riveted to their chair as he taught for nine straight hours. The strategies I learned that day completely transformed my business and my idea of what was possible. In *LAUNCH*, you get the strategies Jeff taught that day, and more. This is the business book of the year, and I'm personally buying a copy for all my top coaching students.

—**JJ Virgin**, CNS, CHFS, *New York Times* Bestselling Author of *The Virgin Diet* and *The Virgin Diet Cookbook*

People trust Jeff Walker because Walker has consistently for years been on the forefront of producing results online with his Product Launch Formula. Now he has distilled his system into *LAUNCH* so anyone can learn it, implement it, and launch it! It's almost unfair, how easy he just made it for you. I won't launch another book without using *LAUNCH*. Jeff Walker created the road map, and I plan to use it.

—**David Bach**, Nine-time *New York Times* Bestselling Author and Creator of the *FinishRich* Book Series

We're completely biased about *LAUNCH* because we used Jeff Walker's launch strategies to generate many millions of dollars in revenue over the past four years, all while costing us almost nothing to execute! That allowed us to play bigger and increase our positive impact on our clients all over the world.

—**Bob and Susan Negen**, Founders of Whizbang Training

I've read a lot of marketing and business books . . . and most of them spend 300 pages to get to one worthwhile idea. This is a serious, practical, comprehensive guide for the real world business owner. If you've ever wondered how to start your business or find more customers online, *LAUNCH* will help get you where you want to go.

—**Sonia Simone**, Cofounder of Copyblogger Media

If I could recommend only one book on how to start, build, and grow an online business, *LAUNCH* would be that book.

—**Ray Edwards**, Founder and Publisher of RayEdwards.com

While so many Internet marketers make bold promises, Jeff Walker quietly produces real results. This book will change how you think about marketing forever.

—**John Jantsch**, Author of *Duct Tape Marketing* and *Duct Tape Selling*

For anyone who yearns to be free of the 8-to-late grind, Jeff Walker is a map maker. Many books claim to offer a roadmap to success. *LAUNCH* really does. If you dream of turning your love of dogs or sports or wellness or just about any passion into a portable business that pays the bills AND feeds your soul, then you need to read this book.

—**Valerie Young**, Dreamer in Residence of ChangingCourse.com

"What Jeff Walker teaches in *LAUNCH* is vital for modern marketing success. You don't need more tactics or tools; you need smart strategy, and that's exactly what this book delivers."

—**Marie Forleo**, Founder of B-School,
Award-Winning Host of MarieTV, MarieForleo.com

Launch

An Internet Millionaire's
Secret Formula
To Sell Almost Anything Online,
Build A Business You Love, And
Live The Life Of Your Dreams

JEFF WALKER

**SIMON &
SCHUSTER**

London · New York · Sydney · Toronto · New Delhi

A CBS COMPANY

First published in Great Britain by Simon & Schuster UK Ltd, 2014
A CBS COMPANY

Copyright © 2014 by Jeff Walker

This book is copyright under the Berne Convention.
No reproduction without permission.
All rights reserved.

The right of Jeff Walker to be identified as the author of this work has been
asserted by him in accordance with sections 77 and 78 of the Copyright,
Designs and Patents Act, 1988.

1 3 5 7 9 10 8 6 4 2

Simon & Schuster UK Ltd
1st Floor
222 Gray's Inn Road
London WC1X 8HB

www.simonandschuster.co.uk

Simon & Schuster Australia, Sydney
Simon & Schuster India, New Delhi

Every reasonable effort has been made to contact copyright holders of
material reproduced in this book. If any have inadvertently been overlooked,
the publishers would be glad to hear from them and make good in future
editions any errors or omissions brought to their attention.

A CIP catalogue record for this book is available from the British Library

ISBN: 978-1-47114-316-8
Ebook ISBN: 978-1-47114-318-2

Interior design by Bonnie Bushman
Bonnie@caboodlegraphics.com

Printed and bound by CPI Group (UK) Ltd, Croydon, CR0 4YY

Dedicated to my wife Mary, and my incredible children Daniel and Joan, who have been with me for this whole crazy ride (and giving me unwavering support every step of the way). I love each of you with all my heart.

Table of Contents

A Note to the Reader

This book will build your business—fast. Whether you've already got a business or you're itching to start one, this is a recipe for getting more traction.

Think about it—what if you could launch like Apple or the big Hollywood studios? What if your prospects eagerly counted down the days until they could buy your product? What if you could create such powerful positioning in your market that you all but eliminated your competition? And you could do all that no matter how humble your business or budget?

There's a process . . . a formula, if you will, that can get you there. I've created and honed that formula over the last 18 years, and I'm going to share it with you in these pages.

There's no theory in this book. Everything I'm going to teach you is based on real-world results. This formula was created through trial and error, testing, and hard-won experience.

I've personally done dozens of wildly successful launches of my own products. But it's not all about me and my success. I've coached my students and clients through hundreds of launches where I was inside the launch, turning the dials and watching all the data.

You're going to meet some of those students in this book, because I'm a big fan of teaching from (and by) example. You will note that they are NOT hypothetical scenarios. I've read lots of business books that use fictional case studies to explain their methods, but this isn't one of them.

I'm going to give you real-world examples. And I'll go beyond that with audio and video Case Studies you can access on the accompanying membership site for this book. I've also got additional training videos and resources at the site, which you can access here: http://thelaunchbook.com/member/.

I'll just go ahead and admit to a fondness for bragging about my students. I love to talk about them, and I love to celebrate their successes. I do it primarily because it's instructive, but also because they're my heroes. I believe that entrepreneurs are the future of humanity. They're the ones who are driving human progress, creating jobs, and building real value in the world. And that's one of the reasons I'm so passionate about my business—it's all about helping entrepreneurs and would-be entrepreneurs.

I also believe that we are living in the greatest time in history for entrepreneurial growth and opportunity. It's never been easier to get started, and it's never been easier to grow a business. The ability to reach tightly niched markets on a global basis is simply unprecedented. For instance, the first sale I ever made was in a tiny niche market to a gentleman in Switzerland . . . and I did it from the basement of my home in Colorado.

Of course, that's not to say that it's easy. There's plenty of hard work involved, just like in any human accomplishment. This is definitely NOT a get-rich-quick book. But the formula has been proven over and over—it's the roadmap to a fast start for your product or business. After all, if you're going to put in the work, it's nice to know that you're using a proven, tested system.

The results have been staggering. I started my businesses from the humblest beginnings imaginable, and I've gone on to sell tens of millions of dollars of my products. And more to the point, my students and clients have dwarfed my own success—they've sold hundreds of millions of dollars of their own products and services.

The funny thing is, as I reflect back, it all happened accidentally. I didn't set out to reinvent marketing or to become a leader in the industry. In fact, when I started out, I had zero sales and marketing experience. And, to a large extent, that's why I succeeded . . .

From Stay-at-Home Dad to Six Figures in Seven Days

Chapter 1

t was just another mouse click . . . just like the hundreds or even thousands of mouse clicks you make every day. But this was a really important click for me, and I hesitated. My finger hovered over that button before I clicked. Five seconds, ten seconds, and still I waited. The truth is, I was terrified. I had months of planning and years of hopes and dreams riding on that click. In fact, it felt like the future of my family was hanging in the balance.

Little did I know that mouse click was going to start a cascade of events that would change the very face of marketing and business on the Internet. But as I sat there at the home-made desk I had shoved into a corner of my dimly lit basement, there were no grand thoughts of anything more than making a few extra bucks to help support my family. I was using a beat-up old computer, an old-school dial-up Internet connection, and I hadn't held a job in more than seven years. Humble beginnings indeed.

But the real reason that I hesitated over that mouse click came down to one word—desperation. I was desperate for a change. I needed a success. I needed to make some money. I needed to turn my life around. And I had been waiting for (and working toward) this moment for too long . . .

This whole journey started when my wife, Mary, walked through the front door in tears—a moment etched in my memory forever. She had left work in the middle of the work day, and now she was standing in front of me, sobbing from the pressure of supporting our family. Mary could no longer stand having to leave for work every morning before her two young kids even woke up and coming home at night when it was almost time to tuck them in bed.

I had been home taking care of our babies. The politically correct term these days is "stay-at-home dad," but back then we just called me "Mr. Mom," and it was a whole lot less socially acceptable than it is now. Several years before that I had quit my corporate job—a job most people would probably consider a good one in operations management. I was the proverbial square peg in a round hole. I just didn't fit in the corporate world. I didn't understand the politics, and I felt like I was forever swimming upstream when I tried to get things done. I saw myself as a corporate failure. So when my son was about a year old and my wife graduated from the University of Colorado and landed a new job with the U.S. Bureau of Reclamation, I walked away from my corporate career.

I didn't have a plan. I didn't know what I was going to do. I just knew I couldn't keep living in the corporate world.

The whole Mr. Mom thing went on for longer than I expected. Soon we had a second baby, which meant I was caring for two small children. As anyone who has been in that role knows, my days were busy. But I needed to make a change. I needed to figure out a way to support my family, to give my wife a break, and to relieve all the pressure that was crushing down on our family.

And that's what that mouse click was all about—changing our lives, creating a new, more prosperous future. It was about launching a product and launching a business. It was about creating an income and changing my family's fortunes. Never in my wildest dreams did I think it would change the world.

Go Ahead and Quit Your Day Job

When I finally built up the nerve to click the button, the reaction was breathtaking . . . like stomping on the gas pedal of a Porsche 911 Twin Turbo.

That click sent an email from my computer.

The email went to a server based just outside of Green Bay, Wisconsin.

And that triggered an email broadcast that went out to the people who had subscribed to my simple email newsletter.

Within seconds, that email broadcast landed in the inboxes of my subscribers.

The email was very short, containing less than 50 words. But at the end of the email there was a link to an order form on my web site where people could buy a product that I had just created. The product was a simple email newsletter about the stock market and what I thought was going to happen in the market in the near future.

(Actually, to be more accurate, I hadn't even created the product yet, but I'll get to that later on when I teach you about the Seed Launch™.)

Of course, all that took just a few seconds, but every single second after I clicked the "send" button seemed to drag on for an eternity. I felt like I held my breath the entire time. I needed to know . . . would anyone buy my new product?

After 30 seconds I optimistically checked to see if anyone had bought yet.

Nothing.

40 seconds. Nothing.

50 seconds. Nothing.

59 seconds . . . and the FIRST SALE came in!

A few seconds later, another order. And then another, and another, and then three more. Every time I clicked "refresh," there were more orders!

Within an hour, the total sales were over $8,000. By the end of the day, sales had gone beyond $18,000. And by the end of the week my humble little offer had made over $34,000—almost as much as I had ever made in an entire YEAR back in my corporate job.

That was the launch that brought Mary home. It wasn't my first-ever launch (that's a crazy story I'll get to a little later), but it was the one that convinced me that my little, fledgling business could support my family. Within a few months Mary had left her job and came home to stay. We were ecstatic. (We joke that she "retired", but nothing could be further from the truth—in addition to being a full-time mom, she quickly took over back office operations in the business.)

You know, money is a funny thing. For some people, $34,000 is a crazy amount of money—an almost unbelievable number (and for me, it was life-changing). For others, it might not be big enough to get them excited. But no matter what group you're in, if you stick with me throughout this book, I've got some pretty amazing results to share with you.

I didn't know it at the time, but I was just getting started. And I was creating something that would change thousands of lives.

How I Got Rich Helping Thousands of Others Get Rich

So let's get clear on one thing right from the start: This is not a "get rich quick" book.

Yes, what I'm about to share with you has created incredible riches and abundance in my life and in the lives of many of my students. But that money, wealth, and influence didn't magically appear overnight.

There is a method—a formula, if you will—behind all the amazing success. And that's what this book is all about—taking you behind the curtain and showing you that formula.

Along the way, I'm going to introduce you to a world that most people don't know exists, a world where ordinary people are creating extraordinary businesses. A world where people are starting businesses with almost no investment or capital, often launching those businesses from a spare bedroom or their kitchen table. And a world where those people are going from start-up to profits in a remarkably short amount of time.

And then there are those people who own an existing business who are dropping this formula into that business and seeing a breathtaking increase in their sales.

This isn't the world of high-flying, high-tech start-ups where a few geeky programmers get together, work 20 hours a day, try to "get funded" by some venture capitalists, then sell out to Google for $100 million dollars. (Or, more likely, go bust amidst a pile of greasy, old pizza boxes and empty Red Bull cans.)

If you want to go down that road, I wish you the best of luck. But this isn't the book for you.

What I'm talking about is creating a business (or building an existing business) and generating profits right out of the gate. A business with low overhead, low start-up costs, and minimal or no staff. A business that is highly profitable and gives you great flexibility in your life.

And, last but not least, a business that creates great value in the world and allows you to "do good" at whatever level you choose.

I know, it all sounds like the land of milk and honey, right? All beauty and grace? Can't possibly be true, right?

I know, I know.

In fact, I wouldn't believe it if I hadn't seen it for myself, over and over again.

The reality is this: The Internet has completely changed the game for anyone who wants to have their own business. It's now easier, faster, and cheaper to start and run a business than at any time in history.

And if you already have your own business, the Internet gives you the power to grow your current business more quickly and easily than ever before.

And I say all that from experience. I started my first online business in the "Internet Dark Ages" of 1996, and I've been profitable every year since then. Right through the dot-com crash, right through the Great Recession, right through every Google update. I've sold tens of millions of dollars of my products online in four distinctly different markets. And along the way, I've taught thousands of online entrepreneurs how to start and grow their businesses. My students and clients have done more than $400 million in sales (and counting).

And though I generally don't like to toot my own horn, I think it's safe to say that I'm widely regarded as one of the top Internet marketing experts and leaders ever. (I try to stay away from the term "guru," but, yes, some people refer to me as a "marketing guru.")

However, as you're going to learn, it wasn't always that way. I wasn't born with any type of marketing super-powers. Before I started my first online business I had never run a business before. I had absolutely zero sales training and no marketing skills. In fact, I was always the kid who couldn't sell more than one bag of doughnuts for the Boy Scouts fundraiser every year (and that was the bag that my parents bought).

The Rules Have Changed

The world is clearly in the midst of a huge transition. The very nature of our communications and daily lives has changed radically in just a few short years. We live in a more transparent world . . . a world with a seamlessly connected client base that can instantly pull up thousands of reviews about hundreds of competitors. A world with an ever-increasing level of competition for your prospects' attention. A world where the "marketing fog" grows thicker with each passing day. A world that puts ever-greater value on authenticity and congruency.

The rules of business and marketing have changed, and those changes have killed many businesses. But the changes have also created enormous opportunity for thousands of others. If you understand the new playing field, grabbing your prospect's attention and building a relationship with him or her has actually gotten a lot simpler in many ways. And that's what this book is all about.

So whether you're in a time of transition and you desperately want to start a business . . .

Or you're running a department or a profit center at a major corporation . . .

Or you're a solo practitioner or service-provider (such as a lawyer, massage therapist, Ayurvedic astrologer, etc.) and you're sick of the dollars-for-hours shuffle . . .

Or you might already have a successful online business, but your sales are stagnant and you need to inject some momentum into your business . . .

Or you might even be an artist (such as a painter, author, jeweler, recording artist, etc.) and you're struggling to get noticed in a very crowded digital world . . .

The fact is that you need to launch. Every successful product, business, and brand starts with a successful launch. You can't afford to show up slowly. You need momentum and cash flow, because they are the very lifeblood of every successful business.

Million-Dollar Days

After that $34,000 launch, after Mary quit her job and came home to stay, my business just kept on growing. My launches got better and better, and my results got better and better. At that time, my best launch had done more than $106,000 in seven days—all from my home, all with no staff, all with almost zero costs.

These were the "quiet years." There were lots of great things about my business, and I loved my business and my life. I was making more money than I had ever dreamed of, Mary could stay home with the kids and be a full-time mom, we were able to move to my dream hometown of Durango, Colorado (where I could pursue my passion for all kinds of outdoor sports like mountain biking, whitewater kayaking, and skiing).

That all changed, however, when I went to an Internet Marketing Seminar in Dallas, Texas, in February 2003.

When I got off the plane in Dallas for that seminar I didn't think my business was all that special. I figured there must be a lot of people with online businesses who were doing product launches the same way I was doing them. The success I was having was breathtaking for me, but I didn't know that making six figures in seven days in a little one-person business was the type of thing that would stop people in their tracks.

In the next three days at that marketing seminar, as I met lots of new people (and forged some friendships I value and enjoy to this day), I realized that no one else was doing the stuff I was doing. And they definitely weren't doing launches the way I was or getting the results I was getting. In fact, I was shocked when I realized that I had basically invented a new way of marketing—an approach that would eventually come to be known as the "Product Launch Formula®."

One of the people I met at that seminar was a man named John Reese. He's one of those guys you realize is brilliant the moment you meet him, but at that time he was mostly flying under the radar. He was a true Internet marketing expert, but few people knew it at the time.

We stayed in touch after the event and became friends, and I shared my product launch "secrets" with him. In 2004, John put my techniques to work on two launches. The first one was for a three-day seminar he put on. It did almost $450,000 in sales and proved to me that my techniques would work outside my little business teaching people about the stock market.

John's next launch was for a training course on how to generate traffic for one's web site, and this launch was a game changer. It generated $1.1 million in sales in just 24 hours—a million-dollar day! What makes that number even more shocking is that his business was a tiny, micro-business he ran from home with almost no staff or team whatsoever. (I think John had one person helping with the launch and a part-time customer service assistant.)

I was stunned that this new marketing approach I had invented could generate such insane results. But at the time I was still publishing my financial newsletters, and even though I was starting to get regular calls from people looking for help with their launches, I was largely still behind-the-scenes in the bigger Internet business world. I had a wonderful life—living in Durango, running a great business, going skiing and mountain biking with my kids. I was happy behind the scenes and not looking for a spot in the limelight.

But after John publicly thanked me for my help with his launches, the cries for me to consult on launches kept getting louder. And after urging from John and several others (especially Yanik Silver), I decided it was time to publish my work . . . to start teaching others my Product Launch Formula®.

The Day Marketing Changed

I suppose the real test came on October 21, 2005. I had decided to launch my Product Launch Formula training course, and my reputation (and my business future) were on the line. After all, the proof really was going to be in the pudding. If I claimed to be an expert on product launches, I better do an outstanding job on my great product launch, right?

But even though I had made successful launches—and helped others do the same—there was an extra challenge this time. I was creating an entirely new business, starting over from scratch. All my previous success had come from teaching about the stock market. Now I was going to be teaching people how to launch products and businesses online. I didn't have an email list of prospects in this new market, and my old list of stock market investors wouldn't do me any good at all. I didn't have expert positioning in the market; I was largely unknown except to the few people I had helped with their launches. But that didn't slow me down, because I knew how to get around such limitations. (I'll show you how when I teach you about JV Launches.)

So the pressure was on, but by this time I was an old pro. My launch was a crazy success. In the first week I sold just over $600,000 worth of my new Product Launch Formula (PLF) program. And with that launch, I had instantly created a new business and developed hundreds of new clients and a list of thousands of new prospects.

The proof was in the pudding, indeed. :-)

Since then it's been a wild ride. Over the years I've continually updated and revised the Product Launch Formula so that it has evolved into a complete training/coaching program. PLF arguably has become the largest-selling Internet Marketing training product ever.

I have thousands of Product Launch Formula Owners, and many of them have enjoyed jaw-dropping success. It's hard to quantify their total results, but I know that my students and clients have done more than $500 million in sales, and that number goes up every day.

Remember, most (but not all) of those PLF Owners are small, even micro-sized businesses. That's not like Google doing another $500 million in profits. These are mostly tiny businesses, and the impact of those sales are absolutely huge. And I've had many PLF Owners equal my "six figures in seven days" success, and more than a handful have had million-dollar launches.

People have used PLF in every type of market and niche you can think of and realized tremendous success. In fact, it's almost become a hobby of mine to keep track of many of those markets. Here's just a partial list of some of the markets:

dating advice
test preparation
Photoshop tutorials
loan officers
realtors
juggling
college admissions
baseball coaches
mixed martial arts
SAP programmers
knitting
crocheting
mutual fund investing
trading (forex, futures, stocks, etc.)
dressage
real estate investing
learning guitar
training doctors to read ultrasounds
learning piano
business coaching (around the world)

health food

raw food

massage therapy

romance (writing love letters)

personal trainers

medicinal herbs

fiction writing

horse training

pet care

meditation

dog agility training

marching band accessories

tennis instruction

yoga

youth soccer coaching

songwriting

hand analysis

indoor bicycle training

brain science

self-defense

adventure travel

cake decorating

Remember, in the interest of brevity, I gave just a partial list—there are dozens and dozens more examples. Don't make the mistake of thinking it won't work for your business or market.

It's also been used all over the world—I haven't heard from anyone in Antarctica yet, but it's been used on all of the other continents of the world. I have successful PLF students in dozens of countries, and it's worked in more languages than I can keep track of.

And it works with all kinds of products and businesses, such as:

online courses

home study courses

physical widgets

online membership sites

online services

offline services (dentists, tax services, etc.)

estate sales

ebooks

coaching

mastermind and networking groups

consulting

artwork (paintings, jewelry, etc.)

B2B business system sales

non-profit fundraisers

board games

getting people to church

real estate

travel packages

software

apps

Again, this is only a partial list. But here's the takeaway: along the way, Product Launch Formula and my PLF students have completely redefined the way stuff is sold online.

It's been a wild ride. I could never have imagined where that first newsletter I sent to 19 email addresses would lead.

Enough about Me, What about YOU?

So now you know the story behind the Product Launch Formula . . . but what does all this have to do with you?

Can this formula work for you? Can you start an online business using my Product Launch Formula? Or if you already have a business, can it help you grow your business?

In my experience, unless you're selling a commodity (like gasoline or sand) or you're operating an emergency service (like a locksmith or bail bondsman), then the answer is an emphatic YES. I've seen so many PLF

Owners have so much success in so many different fields that almost nothing surprises me anymore.

And in this book, I'll be sharing some of their stories. You'll meet people from many different walks of life . . . people with wildly different products and businesses. Folks like Susan Garrett, who teaches dog agility training. She started using PLF as a complete newbie and has since created an enormously successful business. Or John Gallagher, who sells products about foraging for edible and medicinal herbs and plants. John was on food stamps when he did his first launch, and now he has a six-figure business. Or Will Hamilton, who sells tennis instruction products and has used his product launches to create a strong enough brand so that he now partners with top-level tennis pros.

All of this might sound like magic, or complicated, or just plain unattainable. Well, stick with me, and you'll see that it's not complicated, that it just plain works, and how and why it can work for you.

I've organized the book to follow in a logical progression:

In the first five chapters I'll give you the foundational material, including an overview of the PLF process, along with email lists, mental triggers, and the Sideways Sales Letter™.

In the next three chapters I'll walk you through the launch process itself— including the pre-prelaunch, the prelaunch, and then the open cart.

The final six chapters will be about fitting PLF into your business and your life, including the Seed Launch™ (this is how you start from scratch) and the JV Launch (how you can do those big mega-launches).

Now just to be clear, I'm not saying that PLF is easy or automatic. There is definitely work involved. Like I said at the beginning, this is NOT a "get rich quick" scheme.

But the reality is thousands of people are creating these types of small, underground, highly profitable online businesses. And with Product Launch Formula they are putting together super-powerful product launches (or entire BUSINESS launches) that are creating nearly instant sales and momentum for their businesses.

Sound good? Are you ready to roll?

In the next chapter I'm going to walk through the basic structure of Product Launch Formula, and then we'll walk forward from there. Along the way you're going to see why it's so completely revolutionary, why it works in so many different markets, and why it works for so many different types of businesses and products.

And soon I'll get to the crazy story of how I made more than a million dollars in sales in a single hour. :-)

One more thing: make sure you go to http://thelaunchbook.com/member/ to get all the extra training videos and resources that go along with this book.

Food Stamps to Six Figures: The Product Launch Formula Explained

Chapter 2

J ohn Gallagher was a busy man. He had a wife and two young kids, he was going to school to become an acupuncturist, and he volunteered nearly full-time at the nonprofit Wilderness Awareness School. When you meet John, you're quickly struck by his earnestness and his passion—and that he's not the kind of guy who sits around idle. But there wasn't a lot of time or money to go around, so John relied on food assistance to help feed his family. He never thought he would have to go on food assistance—he wasn't a "food stamps" kind of guy. But he did what he had to do to get by and feed his family. After all, he was sure it would be a temporary situation, because John had big plans. He had the entrepreneurial itch and what seemed like a great idea for a business.

John's passion is foraging for and preparing edible and medicinal plants and herbs, and he had created an educational board game with his wife that taught kids all about herbs. The game would be called "Wildcraft: An Herbal Adventure Game," and it was time to bring the game to market.

Of course, if you're going to create a board game there are some big upfront costs—the minimum quantity you must order is quite large. But John pushed ahead, borrowing nearly $20,000 from his dad and placing an order for 1,500 games. Like so many entrepreneurs before him, he was willing to go deeper into debt to get his business started. Even though more debt seemed like a step backwards, he knew once the sales started to roll in he would be able to climb out of debt.

Then came the big day when the games arrived at his home, and he started to realize just what 1,500 games looked like. As pallet after pallet was unloaded from the semi-truck, his excitement started to turn to worry. The boxes filled the entire garage. Then the spare bedroom. Then the second bathroom, even the shower stall.

But John put his worry aside, because it was time to bring the game out into the world. It was a beautiful game, and he knew it would provide hours of entertainment and education to a lot of families . . . and it was the ticket out of debt and into prosperity for his family.

So John planned a "launch party" and invited his friends and acquaintances and extended community. He wasn't sure what to expect, but there was one scenario he wasn't prepared for—total heartbreak.

John Gallagher with some of his Wildcraft games.

The Entrepreneurial Land of Broken Dreams

Unfortunately, it takes a lot more than a great idea to start a business. In fact, this story is a lot like thousands of other entrepreneurial stories that end with a soul-crushing defeat. We see it all the time: a new store in the mall, a new restaurant downtown . . . suddenly empty and a "for rent" sign in the window. A beautiful new blog that starts enthusiastically but quickly becomes a ghost town, with no visitors, no comments, no new articles. It's absolutely heartbreaking, because that's not just a business—that's someone's dream. It represents hundreds of hours and thousands of dollars invested into a big vision—a big vision that failed catastrophically.

In John's case, the picture was especially dismal. He sold only 12 games at his launch party, leaving him with 1,488 games to sell. John faced a monumental low point in his life. Not only did he feel like he had failed, he was literally surrounded by his failure. He and his family lived in a home stuffed floor to ceiling with all the games he couldn't sell. Those games seemed to stare at him every minute of the day, all day long. Even worse, he didn't know what to do next. He had just dug himself into a huge hole of debt, he was surrounded by unsold inventory, and he had no idea how to even begin to climb out of that hole.

Like so many other would-be entrepreneurs, John had seen his dreams nearly smashed to pieces on the rocks of what I call "Hope Marketing." He created his product and hoped it would sell. And if you know many entrepreneurs, you've probably heard a very similar story before. However, John's story has a different ending . . .

Snatching Victory from the Jaws of Defeat

At his wife's urging, John went to Google and searched for help about launching a product—which is where he found the Product Launch Formula® (http://www. ProductLaunchFormula.com). And then, since my PLF Coaching Program is not inexpensive, he went to his dad and borrowed even more money. (NOTE: I do NOT advise borrowing money to buy any of my training materials. It worked out for John, but it's not a practice I recommend.)

John dove headfirst into PLF, and he intuitively saw that it would be a perfect match for his board game. Within a few weeks he had a new plan for his product launch, and was ready to put it in place. It's worth noting that John spent almost nothing on his PLF-style launch. PLF is all about the method, not sinking a lot of money into the launch. John counted down the hours to his new launch with huge anticipation, wondering if it could possibly meet his newly heightened expectations.

He didn't have to wait long. The results were staggering—and an incredible contrast to his first failed launch. In just his initial launch period, John sold 670 games, bringing in sales of right around $20,000! Even more remarkable, since he spent almost nothing on his launch, nearly the entire amount could go toward paying off the cost to get the games manufactured.

So for those keeping score at home, that's 12 sales for Hope Marketing and 670 sales for Product Launch Formula. That's an increase of 55 times. The game sold for about $30, so translated into dollar terms, the contrast looks even more dramatic: $360 in sales vs. $20,100. Now just to be crystal clear, John didn't spend anything on advertising during his PLF-style launch. He didn't have any new promotional partners. He didn't get any media coverage. He used the same resources and assets he already had, and since his family was on food stamps he clearly didn't have a lot of resources. In fact, he actually started out with a borrowed laptop computer and using the free Internet connection at the local library.

John's success with that first launch was truly remarkable, but he was just getting started. He's now sold more than 50,000 copies of his Wildcraft game, and he's launched many other products, including one of the most popular membership sites in his niche (HerbMentor.com). In fact, what he's done since that first launch makes his initial success seem modest in comparison. I'll tell you more of his crazy story a little later, because it's such a great illustration of how one well-executed launch can set you up in business nearly overnight. But for now let's just say that he's the guy who went "from food stamps to a six-figure income."

One more note before we temporarily leave John's story: the one asset John had in his launch was a small email list—people who had requested that he stay in touch with them via email. I'll get to the magic of having a list in the next chapter. But the quick story is that when you combine any list with PLF, it's almost like having a license to print money.

A Warning about Those Big Numbers

In the last chapter I threw some crazy numbers at you, like how I started from scratch, ran a business out of my basement, and eventually made $106,000 in a single week (with no employees, no physical store, no inventory—nothing but a computer and an Internet connection).

Then I told you about how I taught one friend my Product Launch Formula, and he sold $1,080,000 in 24 hours—again with almost no staff, no office, etc.

Next I just slipped in that part about my business growing to the point that I did more than $1 million in sales in a SINGLE HOUR (when I was still working out of my home and running things by the seat of my pants).

After that I explained how my students and clients have done over $500 million (!) in product launches in all types of markets—selling all kinds of different products—and that many of those students were running micro-businesses with almost no overhead. And now I've shared the story of John Gallagher, who started when his family was on food stamps and went on to build a six-figure income.

In fact, the numbers are all so crazy that I worry that I might lose you. I understand that when you're just getting started, it can be hard to imagine numbers this big. But please remember two things: First, the numbers are all real. And second, I was a complete newbie when I started out. So was John Gallagher and many of my other students.

If you're like me when I began my business, then the odds of you coming right out of the gate and doing a million-dollar launch are probably lower than winning the lottery. It's not going to happen when you first start out. But you need to know this: You can absolutely start from scratch just like I did, quickly build up your business, and quickly grow your results.

I'm going to walk you through my formula for how to do exactly that, but first I have to introduce you to this "hidden world" where ordinary people are building extraordinary businesses—and they're building them quickly and with nearly zero upfront investment.

The "Secret" World of Online Marketing

There really is a "secret" world of business that most people have never heard of—a world of colorful characters, real-world rags-to-riches stories, and nearly unbridled opportunity.

It's a world where businesses can be created from the ether—start with an idea and you could be in business in a matter of days, often with almost no investment.

It's a world where a seat-of-the-pants business that you run from home with a skeleton staff (or no staff at all) can become a multi-million dollar company.

It's a world that's not limited by time and space. You can run your business on your own schedule, and you can pick it up and move it to Hawaii if you like (or the mountains of Colorado, like I did).

It's a world where you don't need to invest large sums of money to get started, where you can "bootstrap" your way to success without having to raise any capital.

And it's a world that "scales"—because these businesses can grow independent of the time you put into them. That means you break free of the trap of trading your precious time for dollars. Your income becomes leveraged. It's a world where someone in the 99% truly can get rich.

This is the world of the entrepreneurial direct marketing micro-business. And I was lucky enough to stumble into it back in 1996, during the earliest days of online business. This world has transformed my life, and I've watched it transform the lives of thousands of other people. The history and evolution of that world is a crazy story, and maybe someday I'll write that book, because it's a story that few have experienced as fully as I did. But more to the point of this book, I'm going to have to bring you into this world to give you a full understanding of the Product Launch Formula and how you can put the power of PLF to work in your business and your life.

But make no mistake: No matter what the size or type of your business (or your business dreams), this world offers something for you.

Way back when I started in 1996, the Internet was expanding like crazy. The growth rate was exponential. Every month the number of users grew by a faster rate. The word "Internet" was starting to enter the collective consciousness, and suddenly everyone was talking about it—even if they didn't quite understand what it was. But no one had really figured out how to use the Internet for business, and the question from every business-minded person was "But can I make any money from it?"

The big corporations certainly didn't have a plan. For the most part, the Internet was more like the Wild West than a normal business environment. And that's not the type of arena the big corporations like to play in. But that's exactly the type of environment the "little guy" (and by that I mean both men and women because MANY of these early startups were run by women) can thrive in. And thrive they did.

The Internet offered the perfect opportunity for the little guy to start a new business. These businesses cost very little to start, there were no set hours (since a web site is always online), and they were independent of physical location. Furthermore, there was no big entrenched competition, there was almost no regulation, you could have an instant global reach, and the Internet was growing every day.

These businesses focused mostly on providing "information" that fell into two categories: information that solved a problem (such as learning to play guitar or installing crown moulding) or content that provided entertainment (such as jokes, photos, games).

When I started my business in 1996, it's impossible to say how many profitable online businesses were in existence, but there weren't very many. My guess is that they numbered in the dozens, or possibly hundreds, but by any count, a pretty small universe. However, that universe or community quickly expanded because people found starting an Internet business to be quick and easy. Of course, the Internet didn't reverse the laws of entrepreneurship—the great majority of those initial businesses didn't last very long. But the sheer volume of start-ups meant a lot of those businesses would actually make it.

And it would be those businesses that pioneered much of the commercial, for-profit Internet world. For instance, I can remember when Jeff Bezos came on a discussion list I was part of to ask about creating an affiliate program for his new online bookstore Amazon.com.

This was the primordial soup of the Internet business world . . . and that's where I created what would become known as the Product Launch Formula.

The Formula That Launched a Thousand Businesses

So by now you're probably wondering, "What exactly IS the Product Launch Formula?" And, more important, "Will it work for me?"

Here's the big picture: The Product Launch Formula® is a system to get your target market so engaged with your product (or business) that they almost beg you to sell it to them. And this all happens before you even release the product.

PLF works in all kinds of markets and with all kinds of products, and it's remarkably adaptable to just about any situation where you're releasing a new product or starting a new business. It's so effective that I've actually had people ask if they could just give me a credit card number to hold on file so I could charge their card and send them the product the instant it was released.

This is the system that I've been using and developing since 1996, and been teaching to clients since 2005. The proof is in the results—the formula just keeps working.

So let's start with a fact we all know to be true: how the growth of the Internet since the late 1990s has changed the world in a fundamental way. It's a very different world, and we're never going back to the old ways of doing things. Nowhere is this more true than in business, and in that arena, we're going to focus on three huge changes:

1. **Speed of communication:** It's a lot easier and faster to communicate with your market than ever before. Within just a few minutes, you can write an email and broadcast it to your list of prospects and clients. They can be reading your message within seconds of when you press the "send" button. A few short years ago, the total time from original thought to creation to publication to consumption would be measured in days or weeks or months. Now it can be compressed to minutes.

2. **Cost of communication:** The cost to send an email or make a post to your social media followers is extremely low. The barriers to entry in the publishing game have been removed. What does it cost to become a publisher? Someone can create a Facebook page or a Twitter profile for free and start publishing instantly. A decade or two ago even the most inexpensive ways to start broadcasting or publishing would have set you back thousands of dollars.

3. **Interactivity:** When your followers respond to your message, you have all kinds of tracking data. This gives you nearly instant feedback on how your message is resonating with your target market. Compare that to a few years ago, when publishing was almost like shouting into the wilderness. Depending on the terrain and other conditions, you might hear a faint echo some time after your shout. Or more likely, you would get no feedback whatsoever.

Perhaps you've never thought about these changes before or maybe by now you take them for granted. Either way, they have huge implications in many areas of our human experience—from politics to entertainment to medicine to interpersonal relationships. But what we're going to focus on here is business. Because those three factors—speed of communication, cost of communication, and interactivity—changed the way business and marketing worked, they created a world where nimble entrepreneurs can generate shockingly successful results in their businesses. And as you'll see, all of a sudden those crazy numbers I've been sharing with you will start to make sense.

Turning Your Marketing into an Event

Have you ever noticed how Hollywood tries to build buzz before a movie is released? First there's the trailer six months before the movie. Then there are TV ads leading up to the movie. Then the actors head out on a tour of the talk shows. And nowadays there's a social media campaign right around the release date.

And how about when Apple releases a product? They always create a massive campaign leading up to the release date. In the months before a new product release, all the Apple fanboy sites are full of breathless rumors about when the release will be, the actual product to be released, and what new features to expect.

Those types of campaigns create a huge amount of buzz and excitement BEFORE THE PRODUCT IS EVER RELEASED. In fact, sometimes the product release becomes an event in and of itself. Huge anticipation surrounds the launch, and people are genuinely engaged and paying attention.

Now contrast that to a normal marketing campaign, what I called "Hope Marketing" earlier. That's where you create a product or open a business or roll out a new ad campaign, and you hope it does well.

Now "hope" is an uplifting word and can be truly wonderful in many areas of our lives. If you're shipwrecked at sea—to give an extreme example— hope can keep you alive while you wait to be rescued. But in business, hope is an ugly, nasty word. A soul-sucking word. You need to take control of your success; to the best of your ability, you want to take chance out of the equation. Don't bank the future of your business on hope.

Clearly, it would be better to engineer your product releases, your business launch, and your promotions so that your prospects are eagerly anticipating your launch . . . right?

That's what's behind those big Hollywood releases and the Apple launches. Wouldn't you love to have instant momentum for your business? Imagine how that type of a start would change your business. Think about how creating massive anticipation for your product—before it's even released—would be a complete game-changer.

Of course, there's only one problem. You probably don't have a budget of millions of dollars for your promotion or a hot-shot creative team. And unless you have the resources and talent of Apple or Universal Studios, it seems like you're stuck with Hope Marketing.

Well, hang on, because this is where the Product Launch Formula has changed the game. Remember those three game-changing factors I mentioned earlier— the decreased cost of communications, the increased speed of communications, and the greatly enhanced interactivity? Those are your keys to the kingdom.

And that's why tiny online businesses, run by ordinary folks like you and me, have built an entirely new playing field . . . and it's a playing field with unprecedented opportunity.

Your Market Is a Conversation

So let's start with a nearly universal truth: people find conversations a lot more interesting than monologues or lectures.

And the evolution of the Internet has basically been one long movement toward increased conversation. Never before in history has it been easier to communicate and converse with more people around the world.

Sure, sometimes when you look at the comments on YouTube, those "conversations" may make you question the future of humanity. Nevertheless, we're clearly conversing with each other more now than at any time in history. And that conversation has carried over into business—and marketing. People are no longer interested in being shouted at from a TV commercial about whatever features your product has.

Actually, they were never interested in that, but now they have more choices, and it's a lot easier to tune you out when you start shouting at them, "Buy my stuff, buy my stuff, BUY MY STUFF!"

So instead of shouting at your prospects, what if you engaged them in a conversation? For instance, imagine you're a beginning guitar player, and an expert guitar teacher that you're following online says something like:

> "Hey, I've got this really cool new technique where I can teach anyone to play one new song each week, and I just came up with a crazy idea to put together a course that teaches my 'secret' method.
>
> (Actually, I don't know if it's a secret, but I've never seen anyone else use this method. I showed it to a few friends, and it works like gangbusters.)
>
> In any case, before I create the course, I want to make sure I really cover everything. So can you help me out and tell me what your #1 challenge is when you're trying to learn to play an entire song?"

It's so simple . . . but asking that question starts a conversation. It definitely doesn't shout out "BUY MY STUFF" to your followers.

Opening a dialogue with your potential clients is an example of what I call "the shot across the bow," and it's a great way to start your prelaunch campaign. And that simple question, modified for hundreds of different markets, has been the start of countless successful PLF-style product launches.

Sequences, Stories, and Triggers

Okay, I just gave you a little example of the start of the PLF-style prelaunch. It might not look all that powerful or special, but you'll see soon enough how that inauspicious start can build into something that almost takes on a life of its own.

At its heart, Product Launch Formula is made up of sequences, stories, and triggers. We'll cover sequences first.

The level of information that each of us is subject to every day is staggering. We've got email, voice mail, texts, social media, TV, radio, advertising everywhere (on my airline seatback tray . . . really?), mobile phones, online chat, etc., etc., etc. The volume of information and data is only expanding and will continue to do so. And the number of marketing messages we see every day is growing just as rapidly.

Of course, our ability to absorb and comprehend those messages has NOT expanded. That means we're all working harder and harder to filter out those messages. We're all actively trying to avoid them, to tune them out. We use technology to filter what we can, and then we simply ignore most of the stuff that slips through those filters.

The military uses a term they call "the fog of war." Well, as a business person or marketer, you're competing in an environment that I call the "communication fog." You have to find some way to cut through that fog or your business will perish. It's that simple.

You can't rely on one single marketing message; instead you need to think in "sequences." Instead of relying on a single communication to make your point, you use a sequence of communications that build upon each other. Our product launches use a series of sequences—pre-prelaunch, the prelaunch, the launch, and the post-launch.

Think about the *Harry Potter* books. Which book release got more attention? The first book or the final book? The answer is the final book, because each book in the sequence gathered more attention and more fans—and those fans were rabidly anticipating each new book in the series.

So let's take a quick look at the primary sequences in PLF:

1. **Pre-Prelaunch:** This is where you begin. You use it to start building anticipation among your most loyal fans. (And I understand that you might not have any loyal fans yet—I'll get to that in Chapter 3.) The pre-prelaunch is also used to judge how receptive the market will be to your offer and to figure out what some of the primary objections people will have. And, surprisingly enough, the pre-prelaunch can even be used to tweak your final offer.

2. **Prelaunch:** This is the heart and soul of your sequencing, where you gradually romance your market with three pieces of high-value, Prelaunch Content. You use your prelaunch to activate mental triggers such as authority, social proof, community, anticipation, and reciprocity. And you do all that while you answer the objections of your market. Typically, you release your Prelaunch Content over a period of 5 to 12 days. The format for that content can vary widely, from video to audio to written PDF reports to blog posts to teleseminars to software (and I'm sure we'll invent a few more formats as the years go by).

3. **Launch:** This is the big day you've been building up to, the day you actually send your product or service out into the world and start taking orders (in PLF jargon we call this "Open Cart," as in "you open the shopping cart"). Your launch is actually a sequence as well, and a very powerful one at that. It starts with the email that basically says, "We're open, you can finally buy now," and continues for a finite amount of time, usually anywhere from 24 hours to seven days, when you finally shut it down.

4. **Post-Launch:** This is the clean-up sequence, where you follow up with both your new clients as well as the prospects who didn't buy from you. The post-launch isn't as exciting as the other sequences, but it's important because that's where you deliver value and build your brand. And if you do it right, the post-launch starts to set up your next launch.

It all sounds pretty simple, right? Well it is. And it's also pure gold when you mix in the power of story . . .

Story: How Humans Communicate

Stories are powerful. They are how humans have passed down wisdom, knowledge, and culture for as long as we've been around. Think back to some of your earliest memories from school, and it's likely that the lessons you actually remember were based in stories. Think of all the world's religions, and you will realize that the vast majority of their teachings are delivered through story.

I'm a logical person, and I love knowledge and facts. That's a world I naturally live in. In this book, I would love nothing more than to give you data, theory, examples, and more data. But look how I started the first two chapters of this book, with my story in Chapter 1 and then with John Gallagher's story in this chapter. And guess what you'll remember from those chapters a week from now? I'm willing to bet that it will be "Mr. Mom doing six figures in seven days" and "food stamps to six figures." That's the power of story.

If you want to make your business and your marketing memorable, then your marketing needs to tell a story. That doesn't mean you have to become a novelist, but you need to tell an engaging story about your products and services and why they matter to your prospect. And you need to communicate that story to your prospects.

There is no better way or better place to tell your story than in your launch sequence. This is one of the hidden weapons of PLF, because the most powerful way to communicate your message is with a story, and the serial nature of your Prelaunch Sequence is a perfect place to tell that story.

It's no accident that most Prelaunch Sequences have three pieces of content. Most movies or novels naturally break down into three parts, and no doubt you've heard the term "three-act play." We're dealing with a structure that has been proven over time immemorial, so why not use that structure in your marketing? And why not base your sequences around it? Even the launch itself has three primary sequences: pre-prelaunch, prelaunch, and launch.

Again, this might seem simple, but it's incredibly powerful stuff. And when you start to layer sequences and the power of story together, then you're creating a powerhouse structure.

The Final Piece of the Puzzle: The Mental Triggers

Humans are funny creatures. We all like to think that we make rational, logical decisions. But it's really not that way. In fact, the vast majority of our decisions and behaviors are based in emotion and mental programming—and then we use our precious logic to justify those decisions.

In fact, there are a number of mental triggers that influence those decisions and behaviors. These triggers are always working just below our consciousness, and they exert enormous influence over how we act.

For instance, if we perceive something as being scarce, we will naturally give it more value.

Or if we consider someone as an authority figure, we are almost automatically more influenced by that person.

Or if we consider ourselves part of a community, we will overwhelmingly act in accordance with how we think the people in that community are supposed to act.

Those are just three mental triggers: scarcity, authority, community. There are many more, however, and I'll cover them a little later. But here's the thing to understand right now: These triggers create enormous influence over our actions. They are timeless, and they are universal. They will not lose their power of persuasion anytime soon, and they work in any language, in any country, and just about any business.

And at the end of the day, no matter what business you're in, you are really in the business of influencing your prospects and your clients. And your launch sequence gives you the ultimate opportunity to activate those mental triggers that will influence your prospects and clients.

Putting It All Together

This chapter was a quick whirlwind through the Product Launch Formula. What I gave you here was just an overview; I'll cover all of this in much greater detail in the following chapters. But for now, you can start thinking about combining your sequences, the power of story, and the mental triggers.

When you layer these mental triggers on top of each other, you're not dependent on any one trigger but combining them to create a powerfully influential message.

Then you embed those mental triggers into a compelling and memorable story that cuts through the marketing fog, a story that connects your offer to the hopes, dreams, fears, and aspirations of your prospect.

And you deliver that story in a tight sequence that turns your launch into a big event that captures your prospects' imaginations and builds anticipation toward your launch day.

Now you've got a formula for an incredible launch.

This is the formula that John Gallagher used to sell 670 games instead of the 12 games he sold with traditional, old-world style Hope Marketing. And it's the formula he's gone on to use over and over to build a serious business in a small niche.

Now before we get into the nitty-gritty of the Product Launch Formula, I have one more critical piece of the puzzle for you. And this one will grow to become your own personal "money machine." I think of it as a metaphorical printing press where I legally print money on demand. And you can have one of these printing presses as well . . .

I'm talking about your email list, and that's what we'll cover in the next chapter.

(P.S.—If you would like to see a Case Study I did with John Gallagher where we went through his "food stamps to six figures" launch in detail, as well as his other launches, you can see it here http://thelaunchbook.com/john.)

A License to
Print Money: Your List

Chapter 3

number of years ago, I remember being at a function at our kids'
elementary school, where I chatted with the mother of one of my son's
classmates. Both of our children were in fifth grade, which meant we
were about six years away from the first college tuition bill. And that's a topic
parents of school-aged kids have on their minds.

Since the other parent knew I had an interest in the financial markets, I
suppose it was natural for her to ask what kind of college savings plan I had for
my kids. My answer wasn't what she expected. This is what I said:

"I don't have any college savings plan at all, because I've got a list."

She stared at me blankly, completely confused, which didn't surprise me.
After all, it was something of a smart-ass remark. But I had answered truthfully.
I wasn't worried about tuition bills, because I knew I had something far more
valuable than a college savings plan. What I had was almost the equivalent of
a license to "print" money whenever I needed it. I had an email list of clients
and prospects, and that list gave me the ability to create income on demand. Of

course, there will always be work involved, but the bottom line is that having an email list is the closest thing you can have to a printing press that will print money for you.

Would you like to have that ability to create income on demand? That's what this chapter is all about.

Let me give you a real-world example from my life. When my wife and I decided to move out of the Denver area, the timing wasn't ideal. My business was just starting to really take off, and Mary had just recently quit her job to be home with the kids. We wanted to move to the mountains, specifically to Durango, a beautiful town in southwest Colorado. However, we thought we would take some time before we made the move; we wanted to adjust to Mary being home. And we were still a little nervous about my business being the sole source of income for the family.

But you know what they say about the best laid plans. Just a couple of months after Mary left her job, we took a weekend trip down to Durango and found the home we wanted to live in. It was our dream home in a dream community. And it was available immediately, and we knew it wouldn't stay on the market very long.

The problem was timing. We weren't quite ready to move 300 miles across the state. For one thing, we wanted the kids to finish out the school year in their current school. Secondly, we would have to buy the home in Durango several months before we sold our home in Denver. To do that, I needed a bunch of money quickly—something like an extra $70,000—for the down payment on the new home.

Now at that point a lot of people would start thinking about borrowing money, either from a bank or possibly from a friend or family member. But that isn't what I was thinking. My first thought was "What type of offer can I make to my email list to raise that kind of money quickly?"

That's the power of the list. It means that you have the ability to create a big payday on demand. And that's exactly what I did. I looked at all the interactions and feedback I'd had with my list, and I sat down and mapped out an offer that I knew the people on my email list would want. I also made sure it was a product that I could create quickly and easily. And then I put together a launch for that product.

That's the backstory behind my first six-figure launch—the first "six in seven" that I mentioned in Chapter 1. The result of that launch was that I did $106,000 in a single week, and of that about $103,000 was profit. And just that quickly I had my down payment for my house.

That's the power of the list (and, of course, a well-orchestrated Product Launch Formula-style promotion).

But again, I'm not some magician. I don't have any superpowers. I put in the effort to create that email list—and you can do the same thing. Think about what it would be like to have that kind of an asset in your business and your life. Think about how it would literally transform every aspect of your life.

That's what this chapter is about—building the kind of responsive email list that gives you tremendous power in your life.

The Golden Strategy

List building is one of the core strategies I always focus on in every business I own.

If you take NOTHING else from this book but an obsessive focus on building your list of clients and prospects, this book will still be worth 10,000 times what you paid for it.

So what exactly am I talking about when I say "list"? This is really simple— it's a list of people who have asked to subscribe to your emails. Typically, you have an "opt-in" form on your site, and people can enter their email address in that form to subscribe to your email list.

Of course, you have to give people a reason to subscribe. It might be to receive a newsletter or get daily updates or learn about daily special deals or find out about new content. But no matter what the promise is, that is the reason they are joining your email list.

For example, I'm an avid skier, so in the winter I get daily snow updates from two ski areas near me. Every morning I receive a short email from each that tells me whether they got any new snow overnight. I'm also a guitar player, so I'm on a couple of lists where I get notices of new guitar tutorials. And I use a Mac, so I'm on a list that sends me updates about new Mac software. Those are just a few examples, but I'm on lots of other email lists. I'm sure you're on several as well.

And make no mistake—once you start to build an email list for your business, you've taken a huge step toward controlling your own financial destiny. Of course, this is true no matter what type of business you're in. Your list or database of prospects and loyal clients is always one of the most important assets in your business. If you own a dry cleaning store, the clients who come in regularly are your bread and butter. If you run a restaurant, the customers who come in every week or every month are the people who keep you in business.

However, the online world tends to speed up and intensify everything, and that's definitely the case with your list. In the online world, your list is everything. EVERYTHING.

In fact, it really is hard to fathom the power of an email list until you have a list and you push that "send" button . . . and then within seconds you start to see the people on your list responding and clicking through to your web site. That power is breathtaking, and once you experience it, you will realize the way you live your life has changed forever.

And, of course, since there is so much data and tracking online, you get to see the results in real time. For larger lists (say lists above 10,000 subscribers), it can actually take several minutes before your email list server delivers all the email. But once the email starts going out, you'll typically start to see the response within seconds. And for really large lists (I have well over 100,000 subscribers, and there are far larger lists out there), you sometimes have to take extra precautions so that whatever website you are sending people to doesn't crash. For example, if I put up a new post on my blog at JeffWalker.com (http://www.JeffWalker.com), I have to be careful. If I send too many visitors at the same time, it can crash the server. What I will typically do is stagger my email broadcasts, so that I mail only a portion of the list every few minutes.

Now I don't want to get too technical on you too early in this discussion, and I don't want to intimidate you. If you're starting out in your list-building endeavors, you're a long way from having to worry about crashing servers. I just mention that to show you the power of having a list. You can actually send so much traffic to a site that you overwhelm the server.

We have a saying in the business that sums it up in four words: "Push send, make money." That's why having a list is like having a license to print money at will. Which, of course, is why I wasn't worried about saving for my kids' college education—because I had a list.

What about Spam?

Before we go any further, I just want to be super-clear about one thing. When I talk about email lists, I am NOT talking about sending spam email. I'm talking about building a legitimate list of people who have asked to subscribe to your emails.

There are many definitions of spam out there, and what is regarded as spam has changed quite a bit over time (and the laws regarding spam continue to evolve as well). But for our purposes, spam can be defined as unsolicited commercial email.

When I talk about lists and list building, it is always email that people have asked to receive. I've been publishing online since 1996, and I have never sent a single spam message. In fact, everything I do (and teach) is the very antithesis of spam.

The reality is that spamming is a very quick way to put yourself out of business. Don't do it. Send email only to people who have requested it.

Your List Is Not a Strategy, It's *the* Strategy

As I mentioned above, list building has been a core strategy for me since I started. In fact, it was the ONLY strategy I had when I started out. I actually began my list building efforts before I even had a web site.

I can't remember exactly why I was so focused on list building from day one, but I quickly realized just how powerful lists were. Those lists have become the cornerstone of everything that I do in my business. Of course, over the years, plenty of other people have figured this out as well. But there's another thing that set me apart from the majority of other people who were building lists, and that is summed up in one word:

Relationship.

That might sound like a funny word when we're talking about your email going out to thousands of people, but the reality is that your email is landing in a lot of individual inboxes. Every subscriber on your list is an individual, a unique person. I know I'm stating the obvious, but many list owners seem to forget this.

I hear them talk about sending a "blast" to their email list—their term for an email broadcast. But think about it . . . does anyone like to get blasted?

Remember that your email is landing in a very personal place—the inbox of your reader's computer. If you doubt how private this space is, just think about letting a stranger browse through your email inbox—not a very pleasant thought for most people. Most of us feel very protective of our inboxes, and because every email you send is landing in your subscriber's inbox, you have a lot of power.

Lots of times I'll go to a conference, and people will come up to me (people I've never met), and they'll start talking to me like I'm a long-lost friend. Sometimes I'll wonder if they actually ARE an old friend I've somehow forgotten. They'll start asking me about the stuff I've shared from my personal life in my emails— about how the skiing or the mountain biking season has been, about how my kids are doing, about how my guitar-playing is going. And that's a good thing, because I want my readers to feel like they have a personal connection with me. That connection is what gets them to open my emails, read them, and ultimately click on the links in those emails.

It doesn't matter how many people are on your list if the emails sit unopened in your subscribers' inboxes. If they don't actually open your emails and read them, then you might as well not bother building a list.

What I'm talking about is how "responsive" your list is . . . and the responsiveness of lists varies dramatically. There are lists out there where 60% or more of the people on the list open the email. That's on the super-responsive end of the spectrum. And there are other lists where less than 1% of the people on the list open the email, which, of course, is on the dismally unresponsive end.

Obviously, you want a responsive list. It's better to have a list of 100 people where 60% of them open your emails (i.e., 60 people are reading your email) than a list of 1,000 where 1% open your emails (i.e., 10 people are reading your email).

So how do you build and maintain a responsive list? Well, there's a lot of strategy (and a little magic) in building a responsive list, but it really comes down to "relationship." And the easiest way to increase the responsiveness of your list is to increase the connection and relationship you have with your list. Remember . . .

1. The size of your list is not nearly as important as how responsive the list is, so your list relationship is extremely important.
2. The entire PLF process you are about to learn is one of the best ways to build your relationship with your list.

What about Social Media?

Of course, there are other types of lists in addition to email. You can also build a list of followers on social media sites, such as on Facebook, YouTube, or Twitter.

But as of right now, email still has the real power. In fact, social media lists aren't even in the same ballpark. In terms of pure response rates, an email subscriber is worth many times more than a social media subscriber. In fact, the latest tests I've seen have shown that email is at least 20 times more powerful than a Facebook list. In other words, an email list of 1,000 people will outperform a Facebook following of 20,000. Of course, that number will vary dramatically in each situation based on a lot of different factors, but the fact remains that email lists are still much more powerful than social media lists.

That might change sometime in the future, and if anything is a sure thing, it's that the mechanics of online business are ALWAYS changing. However, I've been hearing about the death of email since 2003, and it's still generating millions of dollars a year for my business.

Another problem with building lists on social media sites is that you are not in control of the platform. If you build a list on Facebook, you need to remember that the list is actually owned by Facebook, and they can change the rules any time they want. And please note that social media sites DO change the rules and have done so with regularity. Your list will become the biggest asset in your business, and it's much too important an asset to build on a platform that you don't control.

Finally, social media sites come and go. A few years ago Myspace was the big thing. Lots of people put a lot of time into building a large presence there. Now it's pretty much a ghost town. Make no mistake, that WILL happen to other social media sites, so you have to be careful about list building on platforms that might go away some day.

So just to be clear, I think there is value in building lists of followers on social media sites, but you need to be careful. When you build a list on a social media site, you have two big dangers. The first is that the site might change the rules in how you can use your list, or they might close down your account altogether. The second risk is that the social media site might actually lose its reach, and people might abandon it for the next big thing.

A Buyer Is a Buyer

There are several different types of lists, and it's important to understand the differences. Lots of times when people talk about lists, they just throw out a number: "I've got a 30,000-person list!" Well, a statement like that doesn't mean much. So let's peel back this onion a little bit . . .

So far we've talked about two types of lists: email and social media. I also mentioned that as of right now, email lists are much more powerful than social media lists.

Another critical distinction is between "prospect" lists and "customer" lists. The definition is pretty simple. A prospect is someone who has NOT bought anything from you yet. A buyer is someone who HAS bought something from you. In your business you will have both types of lists. And the important thing to remember is that a list of buyers is a lot more valuable than a list of prospects. In my experience, a person on your buyer list is worth 10 to 15 times what a person on your prospect list is worth.

This leads to a couple of key points. First, you want to try to move people from your prospect list to your buyers list (and incidentally, a PLF-style product launch is the best way I've found to do that).

Second, you will treat the two lists differently. You want to maintain a great relationship with both, but if you're going to spend extra time and effort on your list relationship, then the place to spend it is on your buyers list. That usually means spending the time and effort to send them some cool content or a bonus of some kind. I remember ordering from an ecommerce store that would often (but not always) include a little bit of hard candy or some other treat in their packages. I'm sure their cost was just a few pennies, but I still remember getting those extras—and it's been several years since I ordered from them. A little surprise bonus or personal touch can really go a long way. For example, we always send out a handwritten "Thank You" snail mail postcard to our new Product Launch Formula Owners. That's a simple way to stand out and build a relationship.

With an online business, it's really easy to create and send content-based bonuses, like an extra training video or report. This obviously works great for information-based businesses (such as someone selling a product on "learning to play guitar"), but it will also work well for other businesses too.

For example, for that web site that sells "learn to play guitar" courses, they could include an extra video lesson on playing moveable chords or some other topic. But let's say you have an ecommerce store that sells guitars. Well, you could send that same video about learning to play moveable chords. Or you could send a video about the care and maintenance of a guitar.

One key factor is how you "send" the bonus video. You could put it on a DVD and ship it out to your client; that would be the old-school way. You would have the time and expense of preparing, duplicating, and shipping the DVD. And the DVD would probably be put aside and never watched.

Or you could put the bonus video online on your web site (which is extremely easy to do—you can find the Resource Page at http://thelaunchbook. com/resources). This method is simpler, faster, and will cost almost nothing other than the time to shoot and edit the video. In addition, you can send a direct link to the bonus video in your email—a great way to condition people to open your emails and click on your links. After all, if you occasionally send them cool bonuses in your emails, they'll always be looking forward to your next email.

List Getting: How to Build Your List

Okay, now that I've been going on for a while about how awesome lists are, hopefully I've got you sold on the idea that you want to get a list as soon as you possibly can. So here's how to do it.

First off, this is going to be a hyper-abbreviated lesson on list building. I could write an entire book on the topic. And I've actually created an entire course on list building, because it's a rich and deep topic and so important. If you want to take this topic further (and you should!), you can get my List Building Blueprint free at http://thelaunchbook.com/list.

So the first thing you need to do is get clear on who your prospect is—we use the term "avatar." Think of your avatar as your typical prospect, the typical person you're trying to reach. So if you're teaching about golf, you generally aren't trying to reach all golfers; you might be going after school-aged golfers who are trying to get a college scholarship. Or you might be going after 45- to 55-year-old women who are just starting to golf after their kids have gone off to college. Or you could be going after men with handicaps under 10 who want to improve their short game.

I actually don't really know the golf market, so I just made all those up. But you get the idea—everything about your marketing will be completely different depending on which of those three different groups you are targeting.

So this is the deal: Your list building effort is the very sharp end of your marketing efforts. It's the first place where people have contact with you, so you have to get it right. And the very first step in getting it right is understanding to whom you are selling, who your avatar is. The reason you have to get this right is we're going to create what is called a "squeeze page." That squeeze page will have an "opt-in offer"—that's the offer you will make to get someone to join your email list. One way to think of this offer is as a bribe, but an ethical one. You have something of value that you will give to your web site visitor if they join (or subscribe) to your list. Your squeeze page and your opt-in offer will be the key to your list building efforts.

IMPORTANT: As I just mentioned, it's important to get this first piece of your marketing right. In fact, it's critical. This is your lead element in the battle for your business. HOWEVER, you don't have to get it perfect right out of the gate. In fact, no one gets it perfect right away. The good news is that it's really easy to be incremental about this. You get your first squeeze page up, and then you work on improving it.

One of the coolest things about an online business is how much data you get and how easy it is to test things. In the most basic form (and one of the most useful), you create two versions of your squeeze page. Then you use software to alternate which version is shown to your site visitors (check my Resource Page at http://thelaunchbook. com/resources) and watch to see which version has the best response rate. After you have a winner, then you use the winner but create another test to see if you can improve it even more, and so on.

This is called "split testing" or "A:B testing" and it's the key to constantly improving your site's "conversion"—in this case, your conversion is simply the percentage of visitors you get to join your email list.

Again, the important thing to remember is this: Don't worry about perfection when you're starting out. No one gets it right the first time. The important thing is to get the first version done and then improve from there.

How to Get People to Join Your List

So what is a squeeze page? As far as can be determined, this idea was pioneered many years ago by my friend Dean Jackson (ILoveMarketing.com) and has proven to be one of the most significant developments in the Internet marketing world. A squeeze page is a very simple page that gives the visitor a choice of only two options:

1. The visitor can opt in with their email address to get some type of free something (this is your ethical bribe).
2. Or they can leave the page.

By forcing your visitor to choose . . . well, you force them to choose. And you should be clear right from the start that, for most web sites, the majority of your visitors will choose to leave your site.

The fact that the majority of visitors will quickly leave your site can be very painful for a new web site owner to think about. But the reality is only one thing on your site is 100% guaranteed—that EVERYONE will eventually leave your web site. And you need to understand this—if they leave your site without opting in to your list or buying something from you, then the odds of their coming back are extremely slim. And when I say "extremely slim" what I really mean is "no chance at all." If you doubt this, just think about your own actions online. How many times do you ever return to a web site that you visited randomly? Even if you bookmark a given site—even if a site is really cool? Probably not very often; instead, it's a matter of "out of sight, out of mind." Your visitors will be the same. Once they leave your site, they will never think about it again . . . UNLESS you capture their email address. Everything changes if they join your list, because then you can use your emails to drive them back to your site (or any site you want to send them to).

When you start to think about your list building that way, all of a sudden it starts to make a lot more sense to put up a squeeze page and force people to make a choice when they come to your site. Make them either opt in or leave.

If you're still having a hard time wrapping your head around the idea of a squeeze page, here's another way to think about it. Consider the value of a subscriber to your email list. When you're just starting out, this can be a difficult number to calculate, but I will tell you that in my market niche, a general rule of thumb is that a subscriber is worth $1 per month or $12 per year. That's a really rough guestimate, and I could write for a long time about email list metrics and the characteristics of email lists. But let's stick with that $12 per year for this example.

So let's say that you do NOT have a squeeze page, but you have some type of form people use to subscribe to your site. Maybe there's an opt-in box in the right-side menu that says "Subscribe to my newsletter." That's not a very powerful way to convert your site visitors into email subscribers, so you might get only 3% of your visitors to subscribe to your list. That means that each visitor is worth 36 cents to you in the next year. This is how the math goes: Since each subscriber is worth $12 per year and 3% of your visitors subscribe, it's a matter of simple multiplication. In this case, .03 x $12 = $0.36.

Now, let's say you have a squeeze page. You are forcing your visitors to make a choice—either subscribe to your email list or leave your site. With a squeeze page, you're very likely to get a higher rate of conversion to your list. In this case, let's assume you get a 20% opt-in rate. That means each visitor is worth $2.40 in the next year. (Here's the math: .20 x $12 = $2.40.)

That means for every visitor you have, you are losing $2.04 by not having a squeeze page. You are getting only 36 cents instead of $2.40 per visitor. Now, of course, this is hypothetical . . . and there are all kinds of different factors and variables at play here. But the fact is that in many cases, putting a squeeze page on your site is an instant win in terms of web site profitability.

So one of the most important things that makes a squeeze page work is having a really strong opt-in offer (this is the ethical bribe that I mentioned earlier). Basically, this is the honey that you're going to offer your visitors on your squeeze page to convince them to opt in.

So what's the ethical bribe? It all depends on your avatar . . . what do they really want? What are their greatest fears? Their biggest desires? What keeps them awake at night? Going back to golf, if your avatar is an average male duffer who plays one round of golf a week with his buddies, then maybe he just wants to drive further than his friends . . . especially on the first tee.

If that's the case, then a great ethical bribe might be a video tutorial on how to completely crush your drive on the first tee . . . every single time. Or maybe instead of a video, it could be a special report (i.e., a written PDF report).

Getting your squeeze page right is really about getting the ethical bribe right. And it doesn't have to be perfect the first time out, since this is another thing you can test very easily. But at the end of the day, the effectiveness of your squeeze page is very much dependent on the quality of your bribe and how closely it aligns with your avatar's hopes, dreams, nd desires.

Okay, enough theory . . . let's take a look at some examples of squeeze pages.

ProductLaunchFormula.com

ListGettingBlueprint.com

VictoriaLabalme.com

InnerCircleSessions.com/training

So far we've covered:

1. Defining your avatar.
2. Creating your opt-in ethical bribe.
3. Creating your squeeze page.

Now the only thing left to do to get your list rolling is drive some traffic to your squeeze page. Of course, driving traffic is another one of those huge topics that I could write a book or two about. And it's a topic that is constantly changing, which means if I did write those books, they would probably be out of date by the time you read them. But here's a big picture overview . . .

There are a number of ways to drive traffic. The first one that most people think about is from the search engines, such as Google. This is usually called "natural search" traffic—meaning traffic that comes from people finding your site in the search engines. Getting your site to rank in Google (and by "rank" I mean appear near the top of the search listings) is part science and part art, and people devote entire careers to it. One important thing to remember is that it's VERY hard to get a squeeze page to rank well with Google. Nevertheless, natural search is something that I always build into my business at some level.

Another way to drive traffic is through "paid search." Those are the little advertisements you see at the top and on the right side of the Google listings. There are similar ads on Facebook. Those ads are basically sold on an auction basis . . . they're available to the highest bidder. It's actually more complicated than that, but that's a close enough explanation for now. In any case, paid search can be expensive . . . but it's great for testing squeeze pages because you can literally start driving traffic in minutes.

Another way to send traffic to your site is through Social Media, such as Facebook, Twitter, and YouTube. Again, this is a big topic—far too big to cover in any real depth here, but I would have loved to have something like Facebook available when I started out. You can create a Facebook presence in minutes and start gathering followers there almost immediately. You already know that my preference is always going to lean toward building an email list instead of a social media list, but you can use your social media presence to drive traffic to your squeeze page. In other words, you can use your Social Media following to build your email list.

There are many other ways to drive traffic to your squeeze page, such as creating great content that attracts word-of-mouth traffic (this has always been one of my personal favorites), other forms of advertising, and online forums.

And, of course, there's my all-time favorite source of traffic, which is affiliates and Joint Venture partners. This is when other people with lists send you tons of traffic, and it doesn't cost you a single penny upfront—you pay them out of the sales that are generated by that traffic. This is the ultimate shortcut to building a big list fast. In fact, I've personally added more than 50,000 people to my list in a matter of days using this method. But this is an advanced strategy, and we're not ready to talk about that one yet—I'll go into all the gory details a little later.

The Secret to Having a List Is to Just Get Started

Okay, by now I hope I've got you convinced of the power of lists and the absolute necessity of list building in your business. It drives me nuts that there are still people out there who don't do this. The bottom line is that this is all about your bottom line. Your lists of prospects and clients are the biggest asset in your business. In fact, I could argue that they're almost the ONLY true asset for most online businesses.

Of course, since I've started teaching the Product Launch Formula®, the number one question I get is "What if I don't have a list?" Or sometimes people whine about it: "Jeff, that's great for you because you have a big list, but I don't have one."

The truth is that's exactly where I began—with ZERO people on my list. But I went to work building my list. Slowly, methodically, diligently. Some days I would get a single new subscriber, some days I would get none. My efforts gradually started to pick up momentum, and I would get three or four subscribers a day. I kept at it, and soon I was getting 30 subscribers a day . . . and 30 subscribers a day starts to add up. That's 900 subscribers a month or 10,800 subscribers a year.

And guess what? In many markets you can make hundreds of thousands of dollars a year with a list of 10,000 subscribers.

The bottom line is that if you want to build a viable business online, you NEED to focus on list building. That's why I put this chapter so early in the book—it's a core principle. And it's part of the Product Launch Formula story, because there is no better way to maximize the results you get from your list than with a product launch.

And here's an advanced secret: There is no better way to build a list quickly than with a product launch. Remember John Gallagher and the launch of his board game? Well, he had a very small list that he used in that launch. And you'll remember his first launch (before he got PLF) had 12 sales. Then after he applied PLF, he had 670 sales. The one thing I didn't tell you is that in addition to all those sales he made, he also added more than 1,000 new subscribers during that launch.

That's what usually happens in a properly structured PLF-style launch. It's one of the best ways to build your list. But I'm starting to get ahead of myself . . .

The Sideways Sales Letter: How to Sell Your Stuff Like Crazy without Being "Salesy"

Chapter 4

Way back in 1996, when I started my first online business and I didn't have a clue about sales or marketing, I stumbled my way through all kinds of things. And I made one "mistake" that has made all the difference. In fact, that mistake became the core strategy that's made me millions of dollars, made my clients hundreds of millions of dollars, and changed the way stuff is sold online. That strategy is the Sideways Sales Letter™.

Back when I started, I not only didn't have a clue about how to sell stuff, but I didn't even know there were entire schools of thought about selling. I didn't know there were all kinds of sales theory and sales training. I just had no idea.

So I did the only thing that seemed natural: I made up my own way of selling. And it turns out that what I created was perfectly tuned to the new way that business was quickly evolving to. It was perfectly suited to the Internet and our newly connected lives. As people have become exponentially more connected due to the Internet, the entire game of selling stuff has changed.

Think about it. When you buy almost any type of hard goods, you can instantly pull up real user reviews on Amazon.com. You're about to go on vacation, you can quickly look at reviews on TripAdvisor.com. You're looking for an entertaining movie to go to, you can check out the ratings . . . well, pretty much everywhere.

And with greater connectivity, people have become more highly tuned to authenticity. They're more skeptical. It's like everyone is walking around with a giant super-sensitive "BS Detector" that's always on full alert.

People have learned to see a pitch coming a thousand miles away, and they've learned to distrust it. It's just a side effect of our uber-connected world. And that's why, in most cases, the traditional old way of selling doesn't work so well anymore. Or at least not nearly as well as the Sideways Sales Letter does.

Before I can explain the Sideways Sales Letter, I need to give you some context. There's a traditional tool in direct marketing going back many decades simply called the "sales letter" (also known as the "long form sales letter"). Basically, this is a lengthy printed advertisement written in the form of a letter. These sales letters can be eight pages, 12 pages, 24 pages, or even longer. When most people first encounter a long form sales letter, they have one of two reactions. If it's a topic they are interested in and it's a good letter that's been written by a pro copywriter, they'll start reading it and soon get sucked right into the narrative of the letter. On the other hand, if it's a topic they don't care about or the letter is poorly written, they'll wonder why ANYONE would ever read such a long and boring advertisement.

But the important thing for you to remember is that these form sales letters have been used for decades, and they have generated billions of dollars in sales for all kinds of different products. The development of long form copy and the sales letter was one of the most significant advances ever in sales and marketing. It was, to borrow an old phrase from advertising legend Albert Lasker, "salesmanship multiplied." You could effectively make a complicated sale without being face-to-face with your prospect.

An Old Tool for New Profits

So what happened to the sales letter when the Internet came along? Well, it made the jump to the online world pretty easily. In fact, within a few years sales letters became really popular online. In fact, they got even longer on the Internet, because you didn't need to pay for printing. It didn't cost any more to use a 40-page sales letter than a 12-page letter, so the length of many of the letters got longer.

And in the last few years, another change has been the use of video. The long sales letter has morphed into a long sales video. Think of it as a 20- or 30-minute commercial.

You've probably been to a web site with a long form sales letter or sales video. These sites are very simple—there's generally only a single page on the site. That page is a very long page of sales copy for a single product. There are no other links on the site other than a "Buy It Now" or "Add to Cart" button. You either buy the product or you leave.

Alternatively, the page might have a sales video instead. In that case, the page will be very simple, with a sales video that might last anywhere from 15 minutes up to an hour or more. Again, the only link on the page is the "Add to Cart" button.

As ecommerce and online sales first started to get rolling around 1998 and 1999, the use of the long form sales letter really started to proliferate, especially among small, bootstrapping entrepreneurs. And definitely in the "information marketing" world.

As a bit of a side note, this was back when the big online "brands" were in the middle of the dot-com bubble. They weren't focused on conversion, and they didn't even care much about profits. They worried about "user acquisition" and how "sticky" their site was—those were the things that drove crazy valuations on Wall Street. It's hard to believe, but revenue and profit weren't really on their radar for those dot-com businesses. It was the scrappy little solopreneurs and micro-businesses who worried about that type of stuff. And it was those tiny businesses that pioneered the direct marketing techniques that really drive online commerce to this day.

In any case, when the long form sales letter was adopted in the online marketing world, it just plain worked. Many sites that started using this old-school direct marketing tool instantly saw their conversions and profits increase dramatically. But, even as those sites proliferated, their days were numbered . . .

Enter the Sideways Sales Letter™

The secret of the Sideways Sales Letter™ that I stumbled onto was this: Instead of taking eight or 12 or 20 pages to tell the story in a long, vertical sales letter, I flipped the sales process on its side.

Instead of pages, I used days. Instead of a 10-page sales letter, I used a 10-day sequence. Instead of one super-long letter, I split it up into a series of contacts over a number of days. We call those contacts "Prelaunch Content" or "PLC."

Instead of hoping that I could somehow weave such magically spellbinding sales copy that could keep people reading for page after page, I used great sequential content and the power of story to pull the prospect into my sales message.

Instead of delivering the equivalent of a super-long monologue, I turned the whole process into a conversation . . . a launch conversation.

Instead of betting everything on one point of contact when the prospect landed on the sales page, I used the power of multiple "touches" and a sequence to drive my prospects wild with anticipation and turn my marketing into an event.

At its core, the Sideways Sales Letter™ is a sequence of Prelaunch Content, followed by a sales message. The typical sequence will have three pieces of Prelaunch Content, which you share with your prospects over a period of up to 12 days. These days, the content is often online video, but it can take any number of forms, such as email or blog posts or PDF reports. The Prelaunch Content is structured so that it's compelling, valuable content . . . and it naturally leads into the sale of your product. At the end of the Prelaunch Sequence, you "Open Cart" by sending your prospects to a sales page to close the sale.

I want to emphasize that part about **valuable** content—this isn't just about taking a sales pitch and stretching it out over a couple of weeks. That's not going to grab and hold anyone's attention. Through this process you deliver real value to your prospects.

Now, that was a hyper-condensed version of the Sideways Sales Letter and the launch process, and I'll be going into much greater detail on how you do this. But the important thing to get right now is that the results are dramatic. Let's take a look at an example . . .

Stepping off the Work Train and onto the Leverage Train

Barry Friedman is a professional juggler and a highly accomplished one at that. He started juggling when he was 15 and quickly became extremely passionate about it. Barry decided he wanted to make a living as a juggler and entertainer, even though his high school guidance counselor told him he would probably be broke and homeless in a few years. That prediction didn't pan out, and Barry has achieved great success, including appearing on *The Tonight Show* with Johnny Carson by the age of 23 and performing at the White House.

In addition to his juggling skills, Barry also became highly skilled at the business end of his profession. He was able to get high-paying gigs, many of them in the corporate world. Life was good, and Barry was making a great living.

But then came the day that Barry had a nasty mountain biking accident. As he lay in the hospital recovering from the surgery to repair his shoulder and collarbone, he wondered just how he was going to make a living. His career depended on being able to fly around the country to various gigs and performing on stage. Now he was facing six months of recovery, and even then it was unclear whether he would be able to juggle with his surgically repaired body. His income was based on his health and his ability to keep getting up on stage.

Of course, in that regard, Barry was no different than almost anyone else. His financial security was tied to his ability to continue working. Even though getting up on stage and performing was a lot more glamorous than driving to work and sitting in front of a computer at a cubicle, he was still trading his time for dollars. Even though he worked for himself, and even though every show brought a large payday, he was still selling his time for money. If he didn't show up, he didn't get paid.

And that was when Barry started to put together another plan—an alternate way to make a living that would completely sidestep the "trading dollars for hours" way of making money. He was about to step onto what I call the "Leverage Train," where his income wasn't tied to the number of hours or days he worked. Barry knew that many of his fellow entertainers really struggled with the business end of things. They didn't market themselves well, and booking gigs never came easy. And that was something that Barry was very good at—because in addition to being a world-class juggler, he had always been great at getting gigs, especially high-paying corporate ones. He knew how to sell his services and get paid top dollar.

That's when Barry decided to start teaching those skills. He had seen a lot of online training programs, and it seemed like a perfect way for him to teach entertainers how to land more high-paying gigs. Barry had also discovered Product Launch Formula, and he had gone through the program. He created an online membership site called "Get More Corporate Gigs" where his clients could get ongoing training for a monthly subscription fee of $37.

Product Launch Formula works really well for membership sites like Barry's, but I want to focus on the launch of Barry's next product. He decided to create a high-end coaching group where he would work a lot more closely with clients for a much higher fee.

Barry had seen high-end coaching programs (like my Product Launch Formula), and he knew how powerful they could be. So he created an offer for the "Showbiz Blueprint." This would be a 10-week, small-group coaching program where his clients would have access to weekly group coaching calls. There would also be "hot seats" for each participant, a private community site, weekly "office hours," and a number of other benefits. In order to insure that everyone got enough individual attention, the offer would be limited to only 15 participants. The price was $2,000 if people paid in full upfront and slightly more if they used his payment plan.

The Showbiz Blueprint obviously offered a much higher level of training, coaching, and interactivity than Barry's membership site, and it was aimed at the premium end of his market. This type of premium offer is ideally suited to a PLF-style launch, because buying something like this is a big decision and a big commitment. The Sideways Sales Letter gives you the luxury of time to communicate the true value of your offer.

Barry went into this launch with a list of fewer than 1,000 people. He used his first piece of Prelaunch Content to quickly build rapport with his readers and demonstrate that he really understood their pain. In fact, he more than understood their pain . . . he had actually lived it.

He knew his target audience was really good at getting free gigs like library events, festivals, birthday parties, and the like, but they didn't know how to properly market to clients who had money! And they weren't even aware that the marketing they were using to land the low-paying shows was actually driving away potential high-paying gigs.

The real pain point that Barry addressed in his prelaunch (i.e., his Sideways Sales Letter) is that the average entertainer is terrified that they might be forced to get a real job. It's a nightmare for someone who is a talented magician, ventriloquist, comedian, or juggler to think they might end up waiting tables or driving a truck. And possibly even worse—that they would be forced to acknowledge that their parents or teachers or friends were right—they couldn't make a living as an entertainer!

So Barry's first piece of Prelaunch Content showed his prospects that he really understood them, because he had the same hopes, dreams, and fears as they did. And then the video went on to paint the opportunity for them to build a serious business (and income) with their skills. The basic theme of the video was this:

"I'm a lot like you. I found a passion for juggling when I was a kid but was told I couldn't do it for a living. My high school guidance counselor, Mr. Pavliga, said that if I continued to pursue a career as a juggler, that by the

Barry Friedman

time I was 22 I would be broke and probably homeless. Right then, I swore to myself that I would prove him wrong.

"A few years later, I had just turned 23 when I performed on my first *Tonight Show*. I was standing behind the curtain and thinking, 'I hope Mr. Pavliga is watching.' It was all I could think about while I heard Johnny Carson introducing my partner and me. I was told I'd never make it as a professional juggler, but I didn't listen to them and now I've been on over 100 television shows . . . and you can do that too! Now, I want to show you how."

Of course, there was a lot more to the video, but that gives you the overall tone. Basically, Barry was establishing his credibility, he was creating great affinity with his prospects, and he was delivering a very inspirational message. He was also delivering real value, because he was showing his viewers that it really was possible to get great, high-paying gigs. It showed that selling yourself as a highly paid entertainer was a learnable skill. Finally, the video showed entertainers that they had the opportunity to take the same skills they already had, and get paid a lot more money for them. And nowhere in the video was there any hint of a sales message or a pitch. You can see Barry's first video at this link: http://thelaunchbook.com/barry.

One really important part of the Sideways Sales Letter is what I call the "Launch Conversation," because when you post your Prelaunch Content, you will generally do it on a blog where there's a place to leave comments below the video. At the end of your videos you ask for your viewers to respond in some way, such as asking questions and making comments. Barry did exactly that, then took part in the discussion. He answered questions and engaged with his prospects. When you do that, you begin to change your launch from a monologue into a conversation . . . and conversations are almost always a lot more interesting than monologues.

And those comments also give you some incredible insight into what your prospects are thinking and feeling. Their questions will help you identify the biggest objections, which gives you a chance to answer those objections, both in your comments and in your subsequent pieces of Prelaunch Content.

In Barry's second prelaunch video, he revisited the potential pain of failing at the business, then he really focused on teaching. The overall basic message was this:

"What if this all falls apart and your parents were right? What if you can't make it as an entertainer? If you want to make it in this business, you need to treat it like a business. You've spent hundreds of hours working on your craft, but that's only part of the equation. It's not enough to be able to put on a great show. You also need to work on mastering the business. You need to master how to market and promote yourself.

"I've figured out how to do both—put on a great show and build a great business. Here's what I did to build my hugely successful career as a juggler.

Here's what works and what doesn't work. And if you're making these common mistakes, here's how you fix them."

And at that point Barry started teaching his audience the fundamental principles and methods of marketing themselves as entertainers.

Lots of times people worry about giving away too much of the "good stuff" during their prelaunch. They worry that if they give away too much, their prospects won't need to buy their products. But in my experience this is rarely a problem. The mistake I see far more often is not giving away enough high-quality content. In this case, Barry's launch was for a super-premium offer; no one else in the market was charging anywhere near $2,000. If you're going to sell at the premium end, the best way to attract high-end clients is to deliver massive value upfront. And that's exactly what Barry did.

Remember, even though Barry was a very accomplished juggler, and even though he had traveled the world with his business and had even appeared on TV and at the White House, he was still primarily selling to people who had never heard of him. He had no official credentials when it came to teaching people about business. He had no letters after his name. He had no degrees or certifications. He was going to be teaching from experience (which, of course, makes for the best teachers), but the fact remained he was a complete stranger to most of his prospects.

But by sharing great content in his prelaunch videos, he established the authority he needed. He showed that he had the experience to teach his prospects how to get high-paying clients and build their business.

And just like with his first video, there was no hint of a sale in his second piece of Prelaunch Content. Just solid, great content. Barry was building his authority, and he was building great reciprocity with his audience. (Oops . . . I just jumped ahead a little bit. In the next chapter I'll show you the magic of the mental triggers, which build enormous influence with your audience. Authority and reciprocity are two of those critical and super-powerful mental triggers that I'll cover in that chapter.)

Before I leave the question of possibly giving away too much of the good stuff in your prelaunch, let me say this: If you're worried that lots of people won't buy after they watch your prelaunch, then you're absolutely right. Most of your prospects won't buy. In fact, in almost all launches the vast majority of your prospects won't buy. That's just the way the math works. That's how direct marketing works. However, the ones who do buy make all the difference—after all, how many $2,000 sales did Barry need to make a serious impact on his life? The answer is: not that many.

So in his third prelaunch video, Barry reviewed his launch story and he stepped up the teaching even more. He actually reviewed web sites for various entertainers, and he showed the mistakes they were making. And he showed how those mistakes could be easily fixed.

And then Barry started to make a pivot to the sale. He talked about how he was going to personally guide 15 people through his Showbiz Blueprint, which was the exact promotional system that helped land the highest-paying gigs in the industry, including Johnny Carson and The White House. This was the first mention of an upcoming product, the first hint that there was a sale coming.

Making the pivot to the sale in the final piece of Prelaunch Content is critical, and leaving out that pivot is a mistake a lot of people make. Often people who are putting together one of these launches get so caught up in delivering great content that they don't want to talk about the sale in that final prelaunch video.

When I interviewed Barry for the Case Study about his launch, I asked him about this, and sure enough, he told me he didn't want to put that pivot in there. He was loving the teaching, and his prospects were loving Barry for all of his great content that he was giving them. He didn't want to mess with all those good vibes by talking about his upcoming product. But Barry said, "I decided to just follow PLF, and you told me to put that in there, so I did and the formula worked."

The three videos were delivered over a period of six days. And when Barry opened up registration, he sold out all 15 spots almost immediately for a total of $29,955 in sales. His costs were almost nonexistent—basically just the fees to process the credit card orders.

And between the buzz that the launch built up and the results that his clients got, Barry had enough momentum to fill another entire class after he finished the first one. That meant his total sales were $59,910 . . . and he did that with an email list of fewer than 1,000 people.

That means his revenue was more than $59 per prospect—he made nearly $60 for every person on his email list!

But it didn't end there. Since that time Barry has re-run the very same launch with the very same videos four more times. Each time he has put between 15 and 18 people into his class. After a few launches, Barry stopped offering individual coaching calls for the people who signed up. That meant he took another big step up in terms of leveraging his time. He reduced his price to $997 when he did this, but it meant that each additional sale took absolutely no extra time to fulfill. He was now making sales for no extra work. He had left the "trading hours for dollars" world and jumped onboard the leverage train.

If you do the math, he has now sold out six classes with 15 to 18 people per class. The majority of those people paid $2,000 and some paid $997 for the version without any personal coaching calls. That means Barry has done more than $100,000 in sales with very minimal costs. He did all that while selling a product that provided enormous value to his clients . . . and he didn't have to travel to any shows to do it.

That's the power of a PLF-style launch, and that's the power of the Sideways Sales Letter. It gives you the time and space to connect with your prospects and deliver real value. It lets you cut through the marketing fog and set yourself apart from any competition. And it creates a deadly effective sales machine without requiring you to be a great sales person. And you won't feel like you need to take a shower after you make the sale.

(You can see the full Case Study with Barry Friedman here http://thelaunchbook.com/barry.)

Weapons of Mass Influence: The Mental Triggers

· Chapter 5

When I first released my Product Launch Formula training back in 2005, two things happened . . .

First, people started to use Product Launch Formula and get amazing results—to the extent where people in the business were completely stunned. The results were two times, five times, ten times, even fifty times what they were used to seeing.

And second, many "experts" in the market almost immediately started to predict that all that success would immediately start to die off once the tactics became widespread. They said that PLF was a fad, and people would soon stop responding to the launches. Once everyone had seen one of these launches, it would be a case of "the bloom is off the rose" and the results would quickly fall off.

Of course, that didn't happen, because the results my students are getting today are even better than back when I first started teaching Product Launch Formula. As I type this, we just saw one of the biggest-ever launches in one of the most competitive launch-crazy markets. The verdict is in: PLF-style launches haven't gone away. They've just gotten better as we've refined the model.

Here's what those self-styled experts missed back in 2005, and here's what some of them continue to miss to this day: A big part of the reason the model keeps working is that we have continued to evolve the tactics. But an even bigger reason is that the success of this product launch model is due to the integral STRATEGIES that we use, and those strategies are timeless. PLF has withstood the test of time because it's solidly rooted in the very core of our mental psyche.

That might seem like a big statement in a book about marketing and entrepreneurship, but that's what we've got in store for you in this chapter . . .

I've already teased you with a little introduction to the mental triggers—those things that directly influence how we act and make decisions. They're incredibly powerful, and they act on a subconscious level. These mental triggers have roots that go back thousands of years, and they are present in all of us to varying degrees. And unless there is a fundamental change in the way our brains work (highly unlikely!), these triggers will continue to exert massive influence over our actions.

Part of the power of the Product Launch Formula is that it gives you a canvas on which to activate these mental triggers as you move through your launch. The mental triggers (along with your sequences and your launch story) form the very cornerstone of your successful product launch. Hit these triggers over and over in your Prelaunch Sequence and your Launch Sequence, and you can create a nearly hypnotic spell over your prospects (and even your entire market).

With Great Power Comes Great Responsibility

Before I give you the details of these mental triggers, I have to warn you this is powerful stuff. And, unfortunately, it can be used for evil as well as good. Frankly, I know this knowledge will fall into the hands of some people who will use it unethically. But I also know from years of working with my PLF Owners, that the vast majority of them are really cool people who have and will apply this knowledge ethically and create tremendous value in the world.

My sincerest wish is that you do exactly that—create something amazing and use this knowledge to share your gifts with the world.

Okay, let's get started—here are nine of my favorite mental triggers:

1. Authority

People tend to follow others in positions of authority. Think about doctors in their white coats. For most of us, as soon as we see that white coat walk into the examination room, a certain part of us becomes deferential. We listen to what the doctor has to say and take any advice seriously. We probably feel at least a little intimidated to disagree with anything the person in that white coat says.

This isn't unusual. We often look for others to help guide our decision. Like so many other mental triggers, the authority trigger helps us shortcut the decision-making process. As we move through our everyday lives we have thousands and thousands of tiny little decisions to make all the time. Every action we take requires some level of thought and decision. Following people with authority is a way in which our brain has evolved to make those decisions more efficiently.

If you want to be more influential in your business and marketing, it pays to be seen as an authority. And the good news is that it can be shockingly easy to create authority. When I was a teenager in high school, I learned a very important lesson about authority. Three of my friends and I were driving home after a school football game—just like a few hundred other people—and got stuck in a traffic jam in the parking lot. There were so many cars trying to get out the exit that no one was moving at all. One of my friends, who understood a lot more about authority than I did, found a flashlight rolling around on the floor of the car and immediately knew what to do. He jumped out of the car, turned on the flashlight, and started directing traffic. Actually, he didn't really direct traffic; he mostly just walked in front of our car and waved us forward through the congestion. Seeing the flashlight's beam, other drivers made way for our personal "traffic director" and we drove right out of the parking lot. The only authority he had to direct traffic came from the flashlight. But people saw that flashlight, and they assumed he was in a position of authority. And I learned a big lesson that night: It just doesn't take very much to create authority.

The Product Launch Formula is a perfect tool for establishing authority. As we move through the prelaunch and share high-quality content with our prospects, we create authority almost automatically. When Barry Friedman mentioned being on *The Tonight Show* and performing at the White House, that gave him instant authority. And since he talked about those accomplishments within the context of wanting to help his clients, it didn't come off as empty bragging but instead helped him bond with his prospects.

2. Reciprocity

Reciprocity is the idea that if someone gives something to us, we will feel some obligation to give them something back in return. This is a very important mental trigger and again this is something that goes back thousands of years. In fact, reciprocity is the very basis from which humans were able to create commerce and trade. For trade to occur, there has to be some amount of trust that when we give a product or service to someone, they will complete the trade by "holding up their end" of the agreement.

Reciprocity is a very powerful trigger. For example, in my family we celebrate Christmas, and a very strong part of the Christmas tradition is the idea of giving gifts. And trust me when I say that one of the worst feelings in the world is when a friend or neighbor shows up at your house with a gift for you, and you don't have a gift for them. Whether you celebrate Christmas or not, I'm sure you can relate to this feeling. When someone gives you a gift, and you don't have a way to reciprocate, that triggers something deep inside of you. You want to "make it right," and you look for a way to reciprocate, to give something back.

During a PLF-style launch, you spend the entire prelaunch giving to people. That's what the whole prelaunch is about . . . giving out great, free content. When you give out that content, you're creating a large reciprocity imbalance. The greater the value of your Prelaunch Content, the greater that imbalance. In the end, when you ask for something back, your prospect will have a greater tendency to want to reciprocate. And at the end of the launch, that reciprocation often equates to a sale.

During a prelaunch there will be several cycles of reciprocity, of giving and receiving before you even get to asking for the order. But make no mistake— reciprocity is an extremely powerful mental trigger, and you'll be activating this trigger throughout your entire launch.

3. Trust

Building trust is the ultimate short circuit to becoming influential in someone's life. I'm sure you can think of many times when a trusted friend or parent or teacher told you something that you believed without question because of your relationship with that person. Something that, if a stranger had told you the same thing, you absolutely wouldn't have believed. That's the power of trust.

Obviously, if you want to influence someone, it's much easier if they trust you. If you want to get someone to do something, it's much easier if they trust you. If you want to convince someone to buy something from you, it's much easier if they trust you.

Of course, in business it can be difficult to earn someone's trust. Especially in the current marketing environment, where everyone is completely inundated with marketing messages all day long. Your prospect is getting thousands and thousands of messages. Cutting through that "marketing fog" is hard enough. Trying to actually create trust in that environment is even harder.

One of the easiest ways to create trust is through time. You can probably think of a time when you had a neighbor who seemed a bit different or even strange. You didn't consider them to be a friend and probably didn't even know them all that well. But after you lived next to them for a period of time, and after they proved themselves to be reliable and honest, you developed a sense of trust in them. Time makes it much easier to trust people.

That's one of the luxuries that the Product Launch Formula® and the Sideways Sales Letter™ gives you . . . time. Compared to a normal "drive by" advertisement or sales pitch, these tools give you time and repeated interaction with your prospects. They make building a trust relationship with your prospect much easier than with the old way of marketing.

4. Anticipation

Another super-powerful mental trigger is "anticipation," and this is one of the cornerstones of the Product Launch Formula. In fact, when I first started teaching PLF, many people referred to it as "anticipation marketing."

Anticipation is one of the triggers that allows you to cut through the marketing fog. It lets you grab your market's attention and not let go. Think back to when you were a child and you looked forward to some special day. Maybe it was your birthday. Maybe it was Christmas morning. Maybe it was your last day of school before summer vacation. Time seemed to slow down as the big, anticipated day approached. It was all you could think about. You couldn't wait for that day.

Well, here's a newsflash—all of us are really just big kids. We haven't gotten over anticipating those special days. And if you do this right, your launch is almost like mixing together your prospect's birthday and summer vacation all in one bundle.

Anticipation is closely related to scarcity, which is another super-powerful trigger I'll get to in just a minute, but basically it's the idea that people will want something more if there's less of it available. Anticipation is also closely tied to "events" where you're circling the date on the calendar and focusing all your attention on that date. If you use anticipation right, people will put the date on their calendar and look forward to your launch. It's like you're putting your prospects into your storyline. They can't wait for the next installment, they can't wait to see what's going to happen, they can't wait to get your product.

As with all the mental triggers, when you mix anticipation with the other mental triggers, the power is magnified and the impact is often breathtaking.

5. Likeability

Likability is a mental trigger that you have certainly experienced in your life. The simple fact is that we enjoy doing business with people we know, like, and trust. We are more influenced by people we like than those we don't like.

So how do we become more likable? At the risk of stating the obvious, you become more likable by doing likable things. When you're seen being gracious, kind, generous, and honest . . . well, people will like you more. And the more likable you are, the more influence you will have.

People generally like to do business with other people more than with a large faceless corporation. If you look around, you'll see even the biggest corporations are starting to realize this, and they're doing their best to humanize their message. And in the age of ever-increasing digital communication, we're all looking for increased connection and authenticity.

If you look at what I've already shared with you about the magic of the Prelaunch Sequence, you'll see that a well-constructed sequence will inherently make you more likable. You're giving people great free content, you're interacting with them, you're responding to their questions and comments. All of these actions make you more likable. You're building a strong connection with your market and your clients. And that makes you more influential.

6. Events and Ritual

When you turn your marketing into an event (which is what running a well-executed PLF-style launch is all about), then you instantly make your marketing truly magnetic. People love events, and they get pulled in by them. It makes them feel as though they are part of something bigger than themselves. This is one of the reasons that sports fans get so caught up in the fate of a team. In reality, the people on "their team" are usually made up of a bunch of complete strangers. But watching their team compete becomes an important event in fans' lives.

A big part of this trigger is the idea of "ritual." When people go through an event together, it becomes something of a ritual. Rituals pull people together and create some of the most powerful experiences we as human beings can have. In fact, ritual is a cornerstone for nearly all religion. In the modern Western world, we are somewhat starved for rituals (which, again, explains why sporting events are so important to so many), and that's why this type of experience can be a peak experience for us.

Now, this isn't a manual on how to start a religion or build a sports franchise, but this is powerful stuff that you can tap into quickly and easily. Turn your marketing into an event, and you will transform your results.

7. Community

Community is a very powerful mental trigger. We act in accordance with how we think the people in our community are supposed to act. Where I grew up, in the American Midwest, almost everyone worked hard to have a green lawn in front of their home. The amount of time, effort, and money it took to create and maintain a lush, green lawn was considerable. I think it's safe to assume that not everyone who was working so hard on those lawns did so because they loved growing grass in front of their home. But the social norm of the community was that the residents had well-cared-for lawns in front of their homes, so they tended them very carefully.

If you reflect on your own life, I bet you can think of many communities you're part of. These might be work communities, social communities,

communities of friends, even online communities. And all of those communities have norms that govern how community members are supposed to act. These norms can be wildly different from community to community, but they are very powerful within the community.

But here's something exciting you might not know. While communities may seem large and established and difficult to get going, that's not always true. You can actually build your own online community right in the midst of your launch. Once you get people interacting with you, with your marketing, and with each other, you're on your way to forming a community. Which means, of course, that you can create your own community norms. Those norms could include actions like helping spread the word about your Prelaunch Content, making comments on your launch blog, or "liking" your posts in social media. Or even buying your product.

8. Scarcity

Scarcity is one of the most powerful mental triggers in existence, period. It's simple—when there is less of something, we want it more. And, in reality, it's the *perception* of scarcity that motivates us. If you think about it, the power of scarcity shows up in our lives over and over, in all kinds of different ways. Why do people value diamonds more than other pretty rocks? Because they're harder to find. They're more difficult to cut. There are fewer of them. And they're very expensive.

Same with gold, or Rolexes, or Ferraris.

One of the things that scarcity does is force people to make a decision. The vast majority of people will put off a decision if you give them a choice, especially when it comes to spending money. One of the key objectives you have in your marketing is to force people to make a decision. That's what scarcity does. If something is truly scarce, then a person needs to act quickly before the scarce resource goes away.

To create a well-executed launch, you absolutely need to build scarcity into that launch. There has to be some negative consequence if people don't take action and buy before the end of the launch (for instance, the price might go up after the launch). If you make sure there's always some scarcity built into your launch, it will take your results to a completely different level.

In fact, we often see as many sales in the last 24 hours of a launch as we do during the rest of the launch combined. If you structure your launch correctly, the last-second rush is every bit as predictable as the rush to buy flowers on Valentine's Day.

It's almost like a spectator sport. If you have programmed scarcity into your launch, plan on making a big bowl of popcorn and sitting back and watching all the orders pour in on the last evening of your launch.

Read those last three paragraphs again—because the power of scarcity will transform your results. If you implement nothing else in this book but that one tactic and you absolutely INSIST on using that tactic in EVERY launch you do, it will literally pay you back 10,000 times what you invested in this book.

9. Social Proof

Social proof is another super-powerful trigger. While it can be very hard to create in an old-style marketing campaign, social proof is extremely easy to build into your PLF-style product launch.

Social proof is the idea that if we see other people taking action, then we will be inclined to take that action as well. Typically we take cues from the people around us when we're unsure of how to act. We are social creatures, and it's hard to overemphasize just how completely we are influenced by what we see other people around us doing.

For example, consider this scenario. It's 7PM and you drive into a strange town. You're hungry and you're looking for restaurant. Let's just say the battery in your smart phone is dead and you don't have any way to check restaurant reviews, so you're on your own when it comes to picking a restaurant. You see two restaurants. The one on the right side of the road has no cars in the parking lot, while the one on the left side of the road has six cars. Which restaurant are you going to pick? Most people would go to the restaurant with the cars in the parking lot, assuming that all those people must know something, right? That's social proof in action.

And think back to your smart phone. If your battery hadn't been dead and you could check out restaurant reviews, well, you would simply be checking another form of social proof. You would be basing your actions on what other people say or do.

One more example. Let's say that you want to download a piece of software or an app. You go to download.com or an app store and do a search. There are 30 different software packages that come up in your search. One of them has been downloaded 3.5 million times, one has been downloaded 17,000 times, and the rest have been downloaded just a few hundred times or less. Which one are you going to try first? Most people will start with the one that's been downloaded 3.5 million times. All those other people must know something, right? Again, that's social proof in action.

So here's how social proof applies to your launch. Due to the interactive nature of your launch, you can create all kinds of social proof. When someone new to your site sees other folks making comments on your Prelaunch Content—saying how excited they are about your launch and how they can't wait to buy your product—that is social proof in action, and it's incredibly powerful.

Layering and Sequencing:
Taking Mental Triggers to the Next Level

So this chapter has taken you on a brief tour through the world of mental triggers—these are the things that influence our actions on a very fundamental level all day long, each and every day. These triggers shape our decisions and actions every day. And, more to the point of this book, they shape your prospects' decisions and actions every day.

I've just given you a brief introduction here. In fact, due to space considerations, I've covered only a handful of the mental triggers. The nine mentioned in this chapter represent about half of the triggers that I've identified and use in my PLF launches. If you want to go deeper on the mental triggers, I've got a video for you at this link: http://thelaunchbook.com/triggers.

One of the important things to remember about these triggers is that they are not isolated. Many of them are closely related, and they work synergistically. When used together, the impact is compounded.

For instance, trust and authority are closely linked. It's easier to establish authority when you have trust. And trust is something that naturally flows from having a position of authority. In fact, there is even a well-worn phrase that combines these two—"trusted authority."

Another example is scarcity and social proof. If something is scarce, it's generally because the demand exceeds supply, which implies there is large demand. And if there's large demand, well that's social proof right there. So it's almost like social proof and scarcity are two sides of the same coin.

Another key point about mental triggers is that they are more powerful when you sequence them and layer them on top of each other. And that's where the Product Launch Formula is unparalleled in its power. The very nature of the way we do launches gives you the time and space to use multiple triggers and to have them build on top of one another.

I'll cover this more when we get to the Prelaunch Sequence and the Launch Sequence, including what triggers you should activate at what point in your sequences, but here's a quick example.

Generally at the beginning of your prelaunch you start with a powerful piece of content that sets up the overall promise and opportunity of the launch. When you share strong compelling content at the start of your prelaunch, you instantly develop authority. That authority comes naturally when you publish that content; it's nearly automatic. You will also develop reciprocity when you do this, because you're giving away your great content freely. You have created a need in the receiver to give back to you, which often translates into a sale. You will also have anticipation going for you, as you talk about everything else that's coming up in your prelaunch.

As you move further through the prelaunch, you develop social proof as people make public comments about your Prelaunch Content. These comments can be on your blog or in social media—either way, you start to develop strong social proof. And hopefully your interaction throughout the prelaunch starts to build likability with your prospects (and maybe even a little trust).

Then as the prelaunch nears its end, and you get close to your open cart date, you hit the event and ritual triggers as people start to anticipate your product. This is a natural time to hit the scarcity trigger, when you start talking about your offer and mention the inherently limited nature of the offer.

That's a quick example of sequencing and layering mental triggers, but I hope I've made it clear how powerful these triggers are. And a PLF-style launch gives you the opportunity to use them together to create an exponentially more powerful effect. That truly is the secret magic here, because not everyone responds to the various triggers in the same way. For example, for some people social proof might influence them strongly, while for others trust and authority are important triggers in their decision making. But when you lay one trigger on top of another throughout your sequences, you build a remarkably irresistible promotion. That's the power of Product Launch Formula, and that's why it's been a complete game changer.

Okay, we've covered a lot of ground. We just wrapped up the mental triggers, and we've already given you a solid grounding in the fundamental parts to the PLF puzzle. Now it's time to press the gas pedal to the floor and get to the hardcore, nitty-gritty fundamentals of putting together one of these launches.

And we're going to start with the part of the launch that's almost completely under the radar. This one component, which no one notices, sets you up for massive success. It's time for the pre-prelaunch . . .

The Shot across the Bow: Your Pre-Prelaunch

Chapter 6

A s you go through this book, it will become obvious that there's a significant amount of work and planning that goes into one of these launches. I know, I know . . . I wish it weren't so. But if you want to make a fortune there is always work involved. I figure that if you're still with me, you're not afraid of a little work.

The place where you usually start is with your Pre-Prelaunch Sequence. This is the magic time where your prospects first get an inkling that something cool is coming.

Over the years I've had lots of people try to reverse-engineer the Product Launch Formula process . . . in other words, they watch a couple of launches and try to figure out how the entire thing is put together. The only problem with reverse-engineering something is that there are often parts hidden "beneath the hood." Leave out those key ingredients, and it screws up the whole thing, making a real mess. And one of the areas that's almost always overlooked is the "pre-pre"—because it's the most clandestine.

The cool thing is that it's also one of the simplest and easiest parts of the formula.

The whole idea of the pre-prelaunch is to begin to activate your tribe—or start building a tribe if you don't have one yet. But you're also doing other important foundational work. You're testing the market's level of interest in your product idea. You're trying to surface potential objections so you can answer them during your prelaunch. And finally, you're gathering information to help finalize your product offer. As if that weren't enough, you're doing all of this while setting the stage for your Prelaunch Sequence.

I like to call your pre-prelaunch the "Shot Across the Bow," which is a naval term for a warning shot fired toward another ship. The whole idea is to get the other ship's attention without resorting to an overt attack. Your Pre-Prelaunch Sequence is all about grabbing your market's attention without actually trying to sell them anything at all.

Sounds like a big job, right? Well, there's much to be accomplished in this phase of your launch, which is pretty amazing when you look at how simple and easy the pre-prelaunch really is to pull off.

In general, my tool of choice for the pre-pre has historically been a simple email or two, although these days social media has also become a big part of the pre-pre for many launches. And there have been a few times where I've used video, and sometimes I've thrown a survey into the mix.

The Ten Pre-Prelaunch Questions

When I'm about to head into a launch, and I'm thinking about my pre-prelaunch, these are the top ten questions that are running through my mind . . .

1. "How can I let people know something is coming without having it feel like I'm trying to sell them something?"

As soon as people think you're trying to sell something, their defenses go up. It's like in *Star Trek*—whenever they sensed a threat, it was "Shields up!" When your prospects feel like there's a sales pitch coming, they instantly believe you less and distrust you more. So the idea here is to begin the conversation about your product WITHOUT overtly selling it.

2. "How can I tease their curiosity?"

Curiosity, which is closely related to anticipation, is another powerful mental trigger. It's a hook that grabs people and doesn't let go. If you can start to engage your prospects' curiosity early on, you'll keep them interested for the entire launch.

3. "How can I get their help in creating this product? How can I make this collaborative?"

This is really important, and it's something most people miss. People will support the things they help create. So if you can get people engaged and create the feeling like they're part of the process—possibly even that they're almost co-creators—then you've now moved them from prospects to cheerleaders.

4. "How can I figure out what their objections are to this product?"

You can't sell to people until you overcome their objections to the sale. You can't overcome those objections until you discover what they are. You might THINK you know what their objections are, but you don't really KNOW what they are until you start engaging with your prospects. Unfortunately, most people launch their products without having any real idea what those objections are. With the pre-pre you're going to find out what they are early on—when you still have time to do something about answering and overcoming them.

5. "How can I start to engage my prospects in a conversation about my offer? How can I be engaging and avoid the "corporate speak" that will kill my launch before it starts?"

This is closely related to the first question, which was about letting your prospects know something was coming without being "salesy." The addition here is the "engagement" piece—starting the conversation and being conversational. In other words, this is where you set the stage for the entire "Launch Conversation," where you create a marketing dialogue instead of a monologue.

6. "How can I make this fun and humorous and even exciting?"

Make no mistake. Even though I'm teaching you an incredibly powerful set of tools, your job of keeping people's attention in a crowded market will always be challenging. Think about every second you're engaging them as a ticking "attention bomb." You have only so many seconds where you can keep them engaged. I'm not trying to intimidate you or be overly dramatic, but the reality is that the people you're selling to have thousands of other things battling for their attention. Think of humor or surprise as an instant attention reset. Every time you get your prospects to laugh or smile, it sets that ticking "attention bomb" back to zero, and you've gained some precious extra seconds.

7. "How can I stand out in a crowded market? How can I be different?"

This is related to question #6. Standing out is about getting your prospects engaged and keeping them engaged. I never want my marketing to be like other people's marketing. I want to be different, unique, memorable. There's an old principle that I always keep in mind: In reality, most people (and businesses) are not having much success. At best, they are getting "average" results. I'm not interested in average results, and you shouldn't be either. So don't do what the average business is doing; watch what they're doing, and do the opposite.

It's not very hard to stand out in your market and with your prospects. Just do things a little bit differently than your competitors do.

8. "How can I figure out how my market wants to be sold?"

This might sound like a weird question, because you might think that the folks in your market aren't walking around "wanting" to be sold to. And you're right, they're not. But they are walking around with problems. And they're walking around with hopes, dreams, desires, and fears. They're lying in bed unable to sleep because they're thinking about those hopes, dreams, desires, and fears. They want solutions. And if you have a solution, they certainly want to buy it from you.

9. "How can I figure out my exact offer?"

No matter how much I would like to make Product Launch Formula seem like complete marketing magic, the truth is that you need to create a great offer. In fact, the term that I use for this in PLF is "a crushing offer." Not really a very technical term, but you get my point. If your launch is going to be a success, you need a crushing offer.

And if you have a crushing offer, you're a long way down the road to having a successful launch.

And your pre-prelaunch is a key to creating a crushing offer. Because if you ask them the right way, your prospects will tell you how to create a great offer.

10. "How can this naturally lead into my Prelaunch Sequence?"
Since your launch (and PLF) is all about sequences, all about creating a greased chute that leads right into your launch day, it's only natural to have your pre-prelaunch tie seamlessly into your Prelaunch Sequence.

My Favorite Pre-Prelaunch Strategy
So with those questions running through my head, I looked for an elegant strategy to find the right answers with just an email or two.

Fortunately, I came up with an old standby strategy that works 95% of the time, and it will almost certainly work for you. There are many variations on this theme, but even the most basic version is extremely effective.

So let's just jump into an example. This is a pre-prelaunch that I created all the way back in 2005 for a product I was launching about trading in the stock market. Now before you go thinking this is ancient history and won't work anymore, I want to tell you that my students in the PLF Coaching Program are still having great success using this exact sequence.

One more thing: This example is about the stock market, but understand that this strategy has been successfully applied in all kinds of markets. In fact, my students have used it in markets that ranged from "how to learn guitar" to "how to get more clients for your massage practice" to "how to take care of your pet dog."

"Quick Announcement and a Favor"
This is so simple and so elegant that the casual reader might miss just how magical, how powerful this is, but I'm going to trust that you won't make that mistake.

So I started this pre-pre with a simple email that I sent out to my list. In recent years, I've done something very similar on my Facebook page. This is what was in the email:

SUBJECT: Quick announcement and a favor . . .

Jeff Walker here. We'll be sending your Trading Update in just a little bit. But first I need to ask you a favor . . .

We're really close to wrapping up our long-awaited trading manual. We will be releasing it in early January. But before we do, I have to ask you a couple of questions. Can you help us out?

You can answer the questions here (and get a little more detail on the trading manual) at this link:

http://www.example.com/

Thanks and best regards,
Jeff

Of course, I gave them a real, live link to the survey . . . but that's it. The start of the pre-prelaunch came in a simple, plain old email that was only 80 words long. Just that email accomplished quite a bit. But before we walk through it, let's take a look at the page my readers were sent to if they clicked the link in the email. They landed on a simple web page that said:

Hi,

We're VERY close to finishing our long-awaited Trading Manual.

We have been working on this for more than four years, but we are finally going to wrap it up. We will be releasing it in early January.

This course will be entirely focused on "Support and Resistance." It will include two printed manuals, eight audio CDs, and one video tutorial DVD. It is going to be a complete brain dump of everything that we know about "SUPPORT and RESISTANCE."

We are going to cover all the ways that we use to generate our support and resistance zones, and we are going to show you exactly how we trade those zones.

HOWEVER, we need your help. Before we finalize everything and send it off to the printer, we need to make sure we have covered everything.

That is where you come in. Please take a few minutes to answer this super-short survey—there is really only one thing we want to ask you . . .

What are your two top questions about Support and Resistance that we absolutely NEED to answer in our trading course?

That was it . . . a super-short email that sent people to a super-short survey.

But if we go back to the ten pre-prelaunch questions up above, you can see I hit a bunch of them here.

1. "How can I let people know something is coming without having it feel like I'm trying to sell them something?"

Well, I definitely let people know something was coming, and I did it without any hint of a pitch. I was simply asking for their help. I wanted their feedback on this project.

And that truly is what the email was all about. But it also accomplished a lot of other things . . .

2. "How can I tease their curiosity?"

I did this in a few ways—first just by telling them something was coming that they couldn't get yet. And then, in the email, I told them they could "get a little more detail" by clicking on the link.

And then there's the key phrase "We're really close to wrapping up our long-awaited training manual," which is repeated in both the email and the survey. Just by telling people that the manual was "long-awaited" sets the expectation that people are already curious about and eagerly anticipating this product. And this is important, because "buzz," curiosity, and anticipation feed on each other. So by starting to build in that perception early on, I'm already setting the stage for the build toward a highly anticipated launch.

Was this product really long-awaited? I don't know. But I do know that I had been dropping hints about it for a long time, and I had built up a list of people who had asked me to create this product. And I know that I had been working on the project for a long time, and I was ready to get it launched. That's enough for me to call it long-awaited.

3. "How can I get their help in creating this product? How can I make this collaborative?"

Well, this one is obvious. When my readers clicked through to the survey, I asked them what their top two questions were about the topic. I'm including my prospects in the creation of my product by soliciting their feedback. This is the key sentence:

"HOWEVER, we need your help. Before we finalize everything and send it off to the printer, we need to make sure we've covered everything."

Remember, people will support that which they help create. I'm giving my readers a chance to help create the product.

There's another subtle bit of human psychology going on here. Remember in the last chapter when we covered the reciprocity mental trigger? Well, this might seem counterintuitive, but we're actually engaging the reciprocity trigger here. Now, you might think, "How can there be reciprocity at play here, since you're asking them for a favor?"

Well, stick with me on this one. First of all, remember that the people reading this were on my email list of subscribers—many of them for a very long time. And, just by virtue of my publishing to them every day, they viewed me as an expert or even a "guru."

And now, by asking for their opinion, I am giving them my attention. And the key word there is "giving." By giving my attention, I am building up a little reciprocity in the minds of many of my readers.

Do you see how, with just a short email and a short survey, we're starting to build up a confluence of triggers that will come into play down the road?

4. "How can I figure out what their objections are to this product?"

This one is easy. I'm just outright asking them to tell me their objections in the survey. No, I don't use the word "objections," because people don't think in those terms. But by asking for their "top two questions," they will tell me what their objections are.

When you do this, you'll always find two or three or maybe even four common themes that keep showing up in the responses. Those themes will contain your prospects' primary objections.

5. "How can I start to engage my prospects in a conversation about my offer? How can I be engaging and avoid the "corporate speak" that will kill my launch before it starts?"

First of all, look at the email and the survey. No corporate speak there. Right from the start, the subject line is "Quick announcement and a favor . . . " When was the last time a big corporation asked for a favor in their email?

And as far as starting the conversation—that's what this entire mini-sequence is about. Asking for their feedback starts the conversation.

6. "How can I make this fun and humorous and even exciting?"

Okay, I'm not sure that I hit this one in this pre-prelaunch other than the fact that I'm letting my readers in on something before it happens. I'm letting them into my creative world. It's almost like whispering something to someone in a crowded room—everyone wants to know what you whispered. In this case, I'm whispering to my readers before I announce it to the general public.

7. "How can I stand out in a crowded market? How can I be different?"

The key here is by asking my readers for their feedback before the product was released, I let them become part of the process. And that's absolutely important, because people support that which they help create.

I gave them a small part to play in the creation of the product, and that's a step toward building an army of people who will support your launch and possibly even buy your product.

8. "How can I figure out how my market wants to be sold?"

This is what the survey is all about. In addition to gathering the top objections, the survey will give you all kinds of additional data and information.

If you use a survey like this, it's often good to mix up multiple choice questions with essay questions. You will get a higher response with multiple choice questions, because it's easier to check a box than to type in an answer. However, essay questions will give you quite a bit more insight. And that insight will often tell you how to construct your Prelaunch Sequence and your Launch Sequence. Often I will literally cut-and-paste words and phrases directly from this type of survey and use them in my Prelaunch Content.

There is an old saying in the direct marketing world: "You want to enter the conversation that's already taking place in your prospect's mind." The responses you get to a survey give you the shortcut to entering that conversation. It's hard to overstate just how powerful this is.

9. "How can I figure out my exact offer?"

Again, the answer to this question is in the survey responses. Actually, this survey is just the beginning of the answer to this question. If I'm launching an information or knowledge product, it's often possible to continue to tweak the answer all the way up into my launch, so I'll gather data throughout the pre-prelaunch and the prelaunch to help me fine-tune the offer.

Even if you're selling widgets, it's possible to add information-based components to the offer. For example, in this launch we ended up adding some live question-and-answer teleseminars to the offer. Since the calls are delivered after the launch, it took zero effort to add them to the offer. And that same type of bonus could be added to all kinds of different launch offers.

10. "How can this naturally lead into my Prelaunch Sequence?"
A few days after I sent that first email I wrote to my list again. I thanked them for the overwhelming response and told them how excited I was to have the project almost complete. That continued the conversation about this upcoming product and did so in a way that was not "salesy." I wasn't screaming "Buy my stuff, buy my stuff!" at the top of my lungs. Instead, I was asking my list to join me as co-creators.

That pre-pre also showed them that I was concerned with making this the best possible product, and I was very interested in what they wanted. And I put them in the state of imagining the product as the best possible product for their needs.

$110,000 in My Bathrobe

The great thing about the pre-prelaunch is that it's a beautiful combination of being simple and powerful. It takes some thought and a bit of advanced planning, but the actual execution of your pre-prelaunch can be incredibly simple. Take a look at the example I gave—it took one super-short email and a survey. Writing the email and putting together that survey took about an hour. (See my Resource Page for services you can use to create your surveys at http://thelaunchbook.com/resources.)

There are lots of different ways to skin a cat, and I've used lots of different techniques for my various pre-prelaunches, but this "Top Two Questions Survey" technique is a winner, and I suggest you use it for your first pre-prelaunch. It's a great way to let your market know something is coming and gather some great intelligence about your market at the same time.

This survey gave me some fantastic feedback on what the market was looking for, what my prospects' biggest objections were, and even some of the exact language I would end up using throughout the launch as I built the momentum toward launch day.

That launch was my first time selling a physical product—a series that included two books and a package of CDs—and I didn't have a big fancy publisher behind me. It was just me and my list of email subscribers and a simple little web site.

Opening the launch in my bathrobe at the kitchen table.

In fact, I did this launch from my kitchen table while I was in my bathrobe. Here's a photo my wife took just a few moments after we opened the shopping cart.

I was smiling in that photo, because it was AFTER we opened the cart. But I certainly had a tense few moments waiting for the clock to tick down to the open. And I'll admit that my finger lingered over that mouse button again—just like it does for every one of my launches. I wondered whether I had everything in place, and I wondered what that next click would bring.

It didn't take long to find out . . .

After I hit the send button, it took fewer than four minutes for the first order to come in. The second order came in five seconds later and we were off to the races. In the first hour we had over $27,000 in orders and when we closed down the launch a week later, we had over $110,000 in sales.

And we did it all without any affiliates, any distributors, any outside sales. Just a simple web site and an email list. Of course, there was a lot more involved in getting those sales than the pre-prelaunch. There was more going on than a simple 80-word email and a simple survey. And that's where we're going next—into the heart and soul of the Product Launch Formula. It's time to put together your Prelaunch Sequence . . .

Sell Them What They Want: The Magic of Prelaunch

Chapter 7

Is it possible to improve your tennis game by watching training videos online? Can you replace (or supplement) tennis lessons with an online membership? And more to the point for Will Hamilton, would people pay for online tennis instruction?

That was Will Hamilton's premise when he started FuzzyYellowBalls.com with a friend. Will was just out of college, and he wasn't excited about the long-term prospects of being a tennis coach. So he set up shop in his parents' basement and started a web-based business. The initial plan was to publish videos on YouTube and make money through advertising. But it quickly became apparent that there was no future in that. In a niche market like tennis, there was never going to be enough video views to drive a serious advertising-based business.

So the next strategy Will tried was creating a membership site with instructional videos. He and his buddy priced the membership to the site at $25 per month. But the site languished and sales were slow. After ten months, they were getting close to writing off the whole idea as a failed experiment, closing up shop, and moving on. It seemed like the answer to the question of whether people would pay for online tennis instruction was "No"—at least not at the volume to support Will and his business partner.

That was when Will discovered the Product Launch Formula. And since it was desperate times, Will leapt into action. He put his first launch together in just a few weeks. As he describes it now, that first launch had some rough edges. Will threw his prelaunch together quickly and used only the very basics of the formula.

But as you'll see in this chapter, even if you get only the core principles right, the results can be dramatic. That first launch did $35,000 in sales in a week's time, which was as much as the business had made since they opened the doors ten months earlier. And since the product was delivered digitally, those sales were almost all profit.

All of a sudden, FuzzyYellowBalls.com was in business. The future was clear—and it definitely involved more product launches. For their second launch, Will buckled down and got serious about following the formula, and results nearly doubled to $65,000 in sales. And the next launch did even better—it was their first one to break the six-figure mark. It closed out at $105,000 in sales. Again, these were digital products, so the profit margin was very high.

With each launch, Will and his partner built their list and their positioning in the market. And their launch skills got better. The next launch was for their new Tennis Ninja product, and that one brought in $170,000 in sales. But it also did something else remarkable: It attracted the attention of the agent for tennis pros Bob and Mike Bryan. Twin brothers, collectively called the "Bryan Brothers" in tennis circles, Bob and Mike are arguably the most successful pro men's doubles team in tennis history. And they were interested in working with Will on a product.

The result was *The Bryan Bros Doubles Playbook*, which Will produced and sold as a full-blown course with Bob and Mike. The launch blew away all Will's previous launches, doing a whopping $450,000 in sales. And a few months later, after the Bryan Brothers won Wimbledon and then the Olympic gold medal, Will got a chance to have his photo taken with the brothers while posing with their medals. Here's the photo—Will is the guy in the middle wearing the two Olympic gold medals:

Will Hamilton posing with the Bryan Brothers
and their Olympic Gold Medals

Of course, getting a photo with a couple of Olympic gold medals is one result I definitely can't guarantee you'll get with Product Launch Formula.

But Will's results show you just how powerful a well-executed launch can be. And one of the greatest strengths in his launches are his Prelaunch Sequences. That's what this chapter is all about. Because if you get your prelaunch right, it makes everything else come together.

(NOTE: You can see my Case Study with Will, along with an example of his prelaunch video content, at http://thelaunchbook.com/will.)

Bringing a Gun to a Knife Fight

Okay, now we're really starting to cook. By now you know about the incredible power of Story, Conversation, and Sequences. And you've gotten a solid introduction to the crazy influence of mental triggers. You also learned about the Sideways Sales Letter. And along the way, I've introduced you to some regular people who have enjoyed tremendous success using these tools in all kinds of different markets and with all kinds of different products.

Now it's time to get down to the nitty-gritty . . . the Prelaunch Sequence. This is where it all starts to come together. This is where you banish "Hope Marketing" from your life and finally start to actually engineer your results with a truly powerful product launch. The thing to remember about your prelaunch (and the entire Product Launch Formula) is that it's not a one-trick pony. It's the confluence of all these tools that create an incredible conversion machine for your business. There's an old saying that goes something like "You want to bring a gun to a knife fight." I'm not a big fan of using violent metaphors, but I like this one. It reminds me of that scene from the movie *Raiders of the Lost Ark*, where the hero Indiana Jones is suddenly confronted with a dangerous villain threatening him with a scary-looking sword. Indiana Jones watches the impressive display of swordsmanship, and then pulls out a pistol and shoots the villain. Danger averted. Game over. It's a memorable scene.

Well, that's what the Product Launch Formula brings to your business. It changes the game and tilts the odds dramatically in your favor. And I'm not satisfied to just bring a pistol to that knife fight. I mean, if I'm going to have to fight then I'd rather just go ahead and bring along a machine gun and rocket launcher as well!

Of course, this isn't about fighting and your marketing isn't a war. It's about designing a great offer for a great product that's going to create great value for your clients. But you can't possibly deliver that value unless you can actually make the sale in the first place.

The bottom line is that this launch process is a coordinated, engineered formula that will transform your sales process. There isn't one specific thing that produces the outsized results we're getting. It's the overall confluence of the tools, tactics, and triggers. It started with your pre-prelaunch, and now we're going to really turn up the heat with your Prelaunch Sequence.

Buy My Stuff, Buy My Stuff, Buy My Stuff!

So one of the key cornerstone pieces of the Product Launch Formula is delivering value and building a relationship with your prospect before you ever ask for the sale. It sounds so simple, but it's crazy how few people actually do this in their business. Instead, what happens is people do the equivalent of standing on a street corner, shouting, "Buy my stuff, buy my stuff, BUY MY STUFF!"

The problem is that no matter what business or market you're in, there are tens, or hundreds, or thousands of other people out there shouting just as loudly as you are. They are all screaming at your very same prospect. It's hard to stand out with that strategy, and it continues to get more and more difficult. The deluge of media keeps getting bigger and louder every day. And there will always be people who can shout louder, or shout longer, or sell at a lower price. You don't want to be fighting that battle. That will wear you down, and in the end it's a losing battle for nearly everyone. Even worse, when you're launching a new product or a new business, then you're automatically going up against established businesses with lots of resources. You need to fight a different battle, a battle where you can create a set of rules that are in your favor.

So how do you do that? It's simple. Instead of *screaming* for attention, you *attract* attention by giving value before there is any hint of asking for the sale. My friend Joe Polish has a saying: "Life gives to the givers and takes from the takers." I think that's always been true, but it's never been more true in business than it is today. And the great news is that the Internet turns the economics of giving on its head. Giving is a lot easier and a whole lot cheaper than ever before, because you're going to be giving away "content," and you're going to be doing it online. That content could be written material or video or audio or any of a number of other media, but the bottom line is that it will cost you almost nothing to distribute that content.

Of course, randomly giving people stuff is not going to do you any good. If you're trying to sell coaching services to high-end corporate executives, then sending them a cookbook of vegan recipes is not going to generate much business for you. You need to structure your content into a sequence that naturally builds up to your sale. And that's the very essence of the Product Launch Formula.

Your Prelaunch Sequence

Your Prelaunch Sequence will generally have three pieces of Prelaunch Content (which I abbreviate to PLC). Think of it as a three-act play with a beginning, middle, and end. Each piece of Prelaunch Content has a specific job. Each one needs to stand alone, but all three tie together into one big story arc. You want to avoid just throwing out three pieces of unrelated content, because you're just not going to get the results you want that way.

The framework for the overall story arc is that you start off teaching people about the opportunity for change or transformation. Then you follow that up with some solid teaching, and you show that transformation or change. Finally, you give the "ownership experience." This is where you start to pivot to talking about your product and the impact it will make on your prospective client.

Throughout this entire sequence you are layering in all the mental triggers we covered in Chapter 5. Since you're giving out great free content, you naturally will hit the **Reciprocity** trigger. And by showing your knowledge of the topic and your ability to give great content away for free, you hit the **Authority** trigger. As you move through the launch, you'll naturally start to build **Trust**. And as you gather comments and create a conversation about your Prelaunch Content, you'll start to build **Community**. And since you're taking your prospects through this entire sequence together, it becomes a shared experience that hits the **Events and Ritual** trigger. Then, as you get closer to your launch date, the **Anticipation** will start to build. In fact, you'll find that your Prelaunch Sequence will naturally trip trigger after trigger, because the process is designed to do that. When you do this right, you end up in a supremely influential position, without having to resort to a bunch of sales tactics that feel like they belong on the used-car lot. Instead, you're building influence in the exact same way humans have always built influence. You're just doing it in a hyper-accelerated way.

Now it's important for you to understand that the magic is in the process. Success doesn't depend on you being a gifted copywriter or master salesperson. Of course, it doesn't hurt if you bring either of those talents to the table, but at the end of the day, the Product Launch Formula is something of an equalizer in the marketing world. It's the process that allows people who aren't ninja marketers to put together a super-effective sales process. And at the end of your prelaunch, if you do this correctly, you will have garnered a list of prospects who can't wait for the moment when they can finally buy your product.

A quick word about formats: You'll find that this is a very flexible process. Your PLC can be delivered via email or as blog posts or as PDF reports or audio. But most of my Product Launch Formula Owners have been using video for the last few years. Video has a number of advantages. Our society has clearly become one where most people spend more time watching video than they do reading. And it's often easier to craft a compelling video than to sit down and write a meaty PDF report. And, unless you're a truly gifted writer, it's a lot easier for your potential clients to get to know you and feel like they have a relationship with you via video. Finally, video content often has a higher perceived value than other types of content.

Without getting too technical, I need to mention that there are two primary types of video: screen-capture video and full-motion video. Screen capture is a video recording of a computer screen with a voice talking over it. You can record a PowerPoint-style presentation or record a demonstration of a web site or some software. Full-motion video is like the video you see on TV; it's shot with a camera. Neither one of these types of video is better or worse; each one has its strengths and weaknesses. For instance, some people prefer screen-capture video because they don't feel comfortable appearing on camera. Others prefer full-motion because there's often less prep work involved—if you know your material and you have a rough outline, you could just turn on the camera and start recording.

Since video has become the predominant format for Prelaunch Content, for the rest of this chapter I'm going to assume that you will be using video for your Prelaunch Content. Please remember, however, that you don't need to do video. I've done plenty of great launches using nothing more sophisticated than email.

Okay, let's take a closer look at each step of your Prelaunch Sequence . . .

PLC #1: The Opportunity (or the Journey)

Your first piece of Prelaunch Content (PLC #1) is critical. It has to grab your prospects' attention and draw them in, so it has to be compelling. And it must answer the all-important question "Why?"

Why should your prospect care? Why should they spend their precious time paying attention to you? Why should they listen to you? What can you do for them?

So how do you answer those questions? How do you get your prospects to sit up and listen? How do you get them to care?

Let me give you the short answer. At the heart of every product, every offer, there is some opportunity for transformation or change. If you're selling a training product that will help golfers take five strokes off their golf score, you're offering a transformation. If you're selling a product that will help people meet the love of their life, you're offering a transformation. If you're selling a machine that helps people open the mail coming into their office 380% more efficiently, you're offering transformation.

Some people just don't like the word "transformation" or they don't see it in their offer. That's fine—you can use the word "change" if you want or even "impact." The bottom line is you need to focus on the end benefit that your product will create for your prospect. At the most basic level, you are either taking away some pain from your client . . . or you're delivering some pleasure.

And that's not just true for your launches—that's true in any situation where you're selling anything. There's an old adage among direct marketing copywriters that if you have a hardware store and you're selling drills, you're not really selling drills—you're selling "holes in wood." People want to buy an end result. Doesn't matter what you're selling. People aren't so interested in the actual tool. The tool is just a means to get that result. And that's what you want to sell them.

Here's another way to think about it. If you want to travel to your favorite beach resort, you're interested in getting there quickly, efficiently, safely, comfortably—and for a lot of people, as inexpensively as possible. You probably don't really care exactly what means of transportation you're going to use. Whatever gets you there fulfilling those requirements is fine. If all those factors were equal, it wouldn't matter if you flew on a plane or rode on a train or drove a car. You're buying the destination, not the means of transportation.

Now if you look at why people don't buy from you, the first and most common reason is that they're not interested in what you're selling. For instance, you might have the greatest wheelchair in the world—the most comfortable, efficient, reliable, flexible design in existence. It might even be priced lower than any other wheelchairs in its class. However, if you're trying to sell that wheelchair to someone who doesn't need a wheelchair, then you're not going to make the sale.

The second reason people don't buy is that they don't have the money. They just simply do not have it, and they have no means to get it. That reason is a deal-breaker as well.

The third reason people don't buy is that they don't believe you. You're telling them how great your product is, but they're not convinced. They either flat out don't think you're telling the truth or they think you're mistaken. In other words, they don't trust either your ethics or your competence.

A fourth reason is that they believe you and they believe you're right about the product and that it actually does work. However, they don't believe the product will work for them. Let's say, for example, you're selling some way for people to quit smoking, and your prospect completely believes you and believes your method has worked for lots of other people. But in the back of their head they're thinking, "I know it works for everyone else, but I've tried 15 other ways to quit smoking, and none of them worked for me."

Product Launch Formula isn't going to help you with either of the first two reasons that people don't buy (they don't want what you've got or they flat-out don't have the money), but if you do this right, then it will handle the third and fourth reasons. They're going to believe you. And the first piece of Prelaunch Content is the critical first step.

So here's a general recipe that works well for PLC #1:

1. **Show the opportunity.** Show/tell how their life is going to change with your product.
2. **Position.** Show/tell why they should listen to you.
3. **Teach.** It's important not to just go on and on about the opportunity; you have to deliver value.
4. **Raise objections and either answer them or promise to answer them in upcoming videos.** No matter what your offer is, there will be objections. You need to face them head on.
5. **Foreshadow PLC #2.** Let them know there's another video coming, and spark their desire by revealing some of the really cool stuff that they're going to learn in PLC #2.
6. **Call to action.** Ask for a comment on your launch blog or in social media.

PLC #2: The Transformation

If PLC #1 was all about the "Why," your second piece of Prelaunch Content is all about the "What"—what is this transformation or opportunity and how is it going to change or transform your prospects' lives? PLC #2 is more about teaching; you want to teach some type of tip or trick that is truly valuable.

What can you teach in five to ten minutes that will make an impact on your prospect? How can you start to change their life right now or at least create a shift in the way they look at their life? It doesn't have to be a huge change or huge impact—just get them moving.

For instance, in one of my launches for Product Launch Formula, my PLC #2 was all about the Seed Launch. (You'll learn about the Seed Launch in Chapter 9—it's a way for someone to do a super-quick launch even when they're starting without a list or a product.)

So in PLC #2 I actually teach how to do the Seed Launch. Of course, since that prelaunch video is only about 18 minutes long, I can't teach it as deeply as I do in the actual Product Launch Formula Coaching Program, but I go as deep as I can in that amount of time. And I've had people successfully do a Seed Launch based on that video alone.

Of course, most of my viewers don't immediately go out and do a Seed Launch after they see that video, but I want to give them enough training so that they can at least see themselves doing one. And that's key: If PLC #2 can get your prospect to see themselves having the transformation that you promised in PLC #1, then you've done your job.

Here's the general recipe for a strong PLC #2:

1. **Thanks and recap.** Thank people for their comments and questions from PLC #1, and then give a quick recap of PLC #1.
2. **Recap the opportunity.** You won't spend as much time as you did in PLC #1, but you need to quickly recap the opportunity. Don't ever assume that your prospect has seen or paid attention to or remembered PLC #1. Remember, they've got busy lives and your launch isn't nearly as important to them as it is to you.

3. **Recap your positioning.** You need to remind them who you are and why they should listen to you. But don't take too long with this—do it quickly.

4. **Present a Case Study or do some real teaching.** You need to deliver some real value for your viewer. Teach them one (or more) cool things that they can put to use quickly.

5. **Objection crushing.** Talk about the top two or three objections and answer them. You want to go after your prospects' big objections to the change or transformation that you're promising.

6. **Foreshadow PLC #3.** You need to let them know you have another video coming soon. Build some anticipation for it by telling them a little about what you're going to teach in that video.

7. **Call to action.** Ask for a comment on your launch blog or in social media.

PLC #3: The Ownership Experience

So PLC #1 was the "why" and PLC #2 was the "what." Now in PLC #3 you will start to answer the "how" question.

In other words, you've shown the potential transformation or change—whether it's being able to play the piano or having a greener lawn or learning to meditate. But usually they still don't see how they're really going to have that change in their lives. Well, the ultimate answer is to buy your product, and by the end of PLC #3, they're going to see that answer. But first you need to continue to build value.

One of the important things you need to do throughout your Prelaunch Sequence is to build the excitement and tension. Think of it like a movie or a novel. As you move through the story you have the "rising action," to use a term from your high school creative writing class. That means that the story is clearly building and moving toward a climax. You want your product launch story to do the same thing. As you move through each piece of PLC, you want to keep building your level of pacing and excitement.

So here's the recipe for PLC #3:

1. **Express thanks and excitement.** Thank your viewers for their comments and questions from PLC #2. Tell them how excited you are and how excited all your viewers are. (And if you did a good job in PLC #1 and #2, then your viewers WILL be getting excited.)

2. **Quickly recap the opportunity and your positioning.** Don't assume they remember (or even saw) your first two videos—briefly describe the opportunity, and remind them who you are and why they should listen to you. Don't take too long with this—move through it quickly.

3. **Possibly present a short Case Study.**

4. **Answer the top questions you've been getting.** In other words, you're going to answer the top objections. You want to do this even if you've already raised and answered those objections in your earlier PLC. People raise the same objections in different ways by asking different questions. So go ahead and answer those questions that keep popping up in the comments on your blog.

5. **Explain the big view and how to make it happen.** This is where you step back and look at what's really possible. What's the ultimate transformation or change that your prospect can have in their life if they buy your product? Look at it from all angles and project out into their future.

6. **Pivot to your offer and create a soft landing**. Do this in the last 25% of your PLC #3. By now your prospects have fallen in love with you, because you've given them huge value. And it's time for you to start preparing them for the offer—that's the "soft landing." You don't want to go from being their best friend in one video to a used-car salesman in the next. So you have to tell them that in your next video you're going to have an offer for them, and they need to watch if they're ready to take their transformation to the next level.

7. **Seed the scarcity of your launch offer.** You will want to have some type of scarcity in your launch offer, and near the end of PLC #3 you want to make some mention of that scarcity. You're not looking to hit them over the head with it, because they still haven't seen your offer. But this is a good time to mention that they should be on the lookout for your next email, because this is going to be a limited offer.

8. **Call to action.** Ask for a comment on your launch blog or in social media.

So that's your three-part Prelaunch Sequence. When you do this right, you will build a warm relationship with your prospects, you'll demonstrate massive authority, and you'll create all kinds of reciprocity. And, of course, you'll deliver massive value in every step of the process.

You'll also create a "launch conversation" as your prospects leave comments on your blog. And that launch conversation will create something of an instant community as people start to read each others' comments (and even start to converse back and forth). That launch conversation will also give you some strong insights into your prospects' big objections, and it will give you a way to gauge whether your Prelaunch Content is striking a nerve with your prospects.

Case Study Caution

There is one thing I have to mention here about Case Studies and the law. But before we go any further, I have to clarify that I am most definitely not a lawyer. Nor do I play one on TV. So what I'm about to say is a lay-person's understanding, and you should definitely get an expert's opinion. In addition, as I type this, the latest rules, regulations, and laws are far from clear, and they're still being interpreted.

But the bottom line is that a few years ago, the United States Federal Trade Commission published new guidelines about the use of testimonials—specifically testimonials that have any results-based claims.

In the past, a seller could include a disclaimer that "results were not typical" when publishing any results from their products. That disclaimer is no longer enough. I don't want to go any further in my explanation here, because . . . well, I'm not a lawyer. And there's still plenty of murkiness around this topic.

I bring this up only because I mentioned using Case Studies in your PLC. Where Case Studies fall with regards to results-based testimonials is still unclear as I write this. So if you're in doubt about some part of your sales process or your PLC and you plan to sell in the U.S., you should consult an attorney to see if you're in compliance with the FTC regulations and guidelines.

Your Prelaunch Timing

And now the all-important question on the timing of your Prelaunch Sequence: How long should it be? How long between each PLC? The answer, unfortunately, is that it depends.

I've personally had prelaunches that lasted anywhere from three days all the way up to 27 days. But I wouldn't recommend either of those extremes for your first few launches. I think a good starting point is seven to ten days. And that time is measured from when you release your first piece of PLC up until you actually launch and start taking orders, which we call "Open Cart."

If you're selling a lower-priced product, say a $27 ebook, then I would tend toward the short end—seven days or possibly even five days. If you're selling a higher-priced product, say a $297 training course on getting a job on a cruise ship, then I would move toward the longer end and go with ten days.

A typical seven-day sequence might look like this:

Day 1: Release PLC #1
Day 3: Release PLC #2
Day 5: Release PLC #3
Day 7: Open Cart

A ten-day Prelaunch Sequence might look like this:

Day 1: Release PLC #1
Day 5: Release PLC #2
Day 8: Release PLC #3
Day 10: Open Cart

The important thing to remember is that the timing isn't nearly as important as the Prelaunch Content. Deliver real value, follow the formula I just gave you, and you'll be fine.

One Critical Thing That Makes This Work

Okay, by now you're probably deep into thinking about all the nitty-gritty details on how to make this work. But let's step back for a second and look at the big picture. Sometimes when people first look at this Product Launch Formula process, they think it's a bunch of marketing tricks. A big basket of psychological tactics that cast a spell on their prospects. Now, I won't deny that you can truly cast a powerful spell when you put it all together, but that's not what really makes PLF work. That's not what is going to grow your business over the long term.

The way you put together a great Prelaunch Sequence is by delivering massive value to your market. If you focus on only one thing, it should be creating value for all the prospects going through your Launch Sequence.

That doesn't mean you're giving away the farm. That doesn't mean you're catering to a bunch of freebie-seekers who will never buy anything. It doesn't mean going broke as you use all your resources to give away everything you've got for free.

What it means is giving real content that creates real value for people. Don't just tease them—give them some substance. Teach them about the opportunity in your first PLC, but go beyond the opportunity. Teach real content that people can actually use. Every time I do a launch, I get comments from people who are shocked at the amount of content I give out. With Product Launch Formula, I have hundreds of people who have done successful launches just based on the free material that I've given out during my prelaunch. And I think that's awesome . . . because there's no way I'll ever sell to everyone, so I might as well create as much value as I can as I move through my life.

In the end, your success and the success of your business is going to be closely tied to the amount of value that you create in the world. And putting together a rocking Prelaunch Sequence that delivers lots of value is a great way to create a lot of value—and you won't have to wait long until the payoff. That comes on the launch day when you Open Cart . . .

Show Me the Money: It's Time to Launch!

Chapter 8

S usan Garrett is a very competitive person, and she was in a race. She had signed up for my Product Launch Formula Coaching Program, and her husband didn't know exactly how much money she had spent to join the program. Susan was determined to make enough money to pay for the program before her husband saw the credit card bill. And since she had no list and no product—and the bill would come through in less than a month— she had some challenges.

Susan is a dog trainer who is passionate about helping dog owners and dogs lead better lives. And she's one of the best dog trainers in the world— especially in the hyper-competitive sport of dog agility. In fact, Susan has won more than 25 U.S. and Canadian national championships and multiple world championships.

Her success and her skills helped her build a successful international business as a dog trainer, sending her to Europe, Australia, and New Zealand to work with her students. For someone who had a huge desire to help dogs and their owners, this was exciting and fulfilling work.

But it also meant that Susan (who lives just outside of Toronto) had a grueling travel schedule. And she couldn't help her clients on an ongoing basis; when she gave a workshop anywhere overseas, it was a one-shot deal. So Susan was already looking for a way to cut back on her travel schedule—and then her husband suffered a heart attack.

As so often happens, that health crisis brought their life into focus. Susan wanted to drastically cut back on her travel, but she needed answers to two big questions: How could she continue to reach her clients who were spread throughout the world? And how was she going to replace her lost income if she stopped traveling to give training workshops?

At that point, Susan had created a few training DVDs, but sales had never really amounted to all that much. They provided a nice supplement to her income but certainly weren't going to replace the income from her workshops.

And that was about the time Susan found the Product Launch Formula. She signed up for my PLF Coaching Program in 2008. And since doing so required a substantial investment, she was determined to do a launch and pay for her entire tuition before the credit card bill arrived (and her husband saw how much she had spent).

Of course, there were a few obstacles in her way. The first two, as I mentioned, were that she didn't have a product or a list. And the third was that Susan had almost no technical skills whatsoever. But the one asset she had was an enormous will to succeed—the same will that drove her to win all those dog agility trophies.

So Susan started with her past clients—she had email addresses for about 1,200 of them. And from taking my training, she knew she needed a list host, so she signed up for my hosting service at ProFollow.com (http://www. profollow.com). She was able to get about 700 of her former clients to join her new email list.

Then she pulled together a product—an ebook she based on some old articles she had written. She compiled the articles and formatted them into an ebook, and she priced it at $14.97. Then it was time to launch.

Susan put together a very simple prelaunch. Since she didn't have tech skills, her prelaunch was entirely email-based. Instead of putting together a sequence

Susan winning one of her many championships

of prelaunch videos, she sent out a series of emails that provided real value and led into the sale.

The results were immediate and breathtaking . . . the launch brought in $27,000 in sales. That easily paid for PLF training, and it also set her up in her new business. That successful response also sold Susan on the value of PLF. After all, her DVD sales had never amounted to more than $10,000 in a year, and they required a lot of work to put together—including buying inventory, working with a distributor, and shipping product. This launch had nearly tripled her best year of DVD sales with almost no costs—and she had pulled the entire launch together in a matter of a few weeks!

Of course, that was just the beginning. When you do a launch like that, it's never your last launch. Since that time Susan has built out an entire line of dog training products, and they're priced anywhere from $47 on the low end all the way up to $4,997. She's done a launch for each new product, and her results have gotten stronger with every launch. Susan's training products are completely online, and she has students around the world. She also has one of the most loyal groups of clients I've ever seen in any business, and she's become one of the acknowledged leaders in the dog agility training market.

It's an amazing success story—the business that was started in a few days with a $14.97 ebook (and a vow to pay for PLF before the credit card bill came in) has grown up. Susan now has a team helping her build her business, and they've made the lives of tens of thousands of dogs—and dog owners—a whole lot better. Along the way, Susan's launches have become legendary in the PLF community, and she's had some of the most successful launches in PLF history.

You can see my Case Study with Susan at this link: http://thelaunchbook. com/susan.

An Astronaut's Perspective

Okay, it's time to LAUNCH!

If you made it to this point, you recognize one big component of a PLF-style launch—there is work involved. I wish it weren't so, because everyone is always looking for an "easy button." Well, PLF is an easy button for creating a great sales process for your product, but you have to put in the effort. The results are worth that effort, however, and your launch day is where all your hard work pays off.

It's hard to describe the exhilaration of launch day. This is the day you've been building toward for weeks or even months. Launch day makes me think back to something I did as a kid. I would take a magnifying glass out in the sun and focus the power of the sun on a piece of wood. Eventually the focused sunlight was strong enough to burn the wood. Your launch is similar. You've focused a lot of energy on this day. In fact, that's the entire point of the launch—to get the attention of those people on your list and in your market and have them anticipating this day. If you've followed my formula, you've raised their interest level to a peak state. And naturally, your emotions and energy are going to be in a peak state as well.

You are never going to forget that first time you push the "send" button and open your cart. I have a friend who is an astronaut and has traveled to the International Space Station three times. He's described for me those first few minutes of liftoff in a space launch—that incredible rush of power and acceleration. As silly as it might sound, his account reminded me of the feeling that comes with a well-executed product launch, where you can get a similar sensation of almost unbelievable power and acceleration.

"They're Heeeeeeere . . . and They Want to Buy"

I can remember one launch I helped a client with. We had a strong prelaunch, and we were pretty confident we had a winner on our hands. All the early signs had been good. About 36 hours before launch we started getting a lot of people asking detailed questions about the price and the offer. In fact, on the last day of prelaunch the whole tone of the comments coming in on the launch blog shifted from questions about the content to questions about the offer. That's always a good sign.

But no matter how good a prelaunch is, you always have a few doubts in the back of your mind. You can't help but wonder: Are people going to open their wallets and buy?

Earlier in the morning of that particular launch, we had sent out the sales page link. There was no actual sales page there yet, just a timer counting down to the open. As the visitors to the site sat and watched the timer, we sat and watched the server stats. Those stats told us how many people were sitting on that page waiting to see our sales video. We had stats on how many people were on the site, what page they were on, and how long they had been on that specific page. The numbers continued to climb. With 30 minutes to go, there were 100 people sitting on that page, waiting for us to open. With 20 minutes to go, 300 people. With ten minutes, we were up to 600.

That's when we saw the load on our server begin to kick up, because the people on the page were starting to hit the refresh button in their web browser. They couldn't wait until we loaded the sales page. Right about then I sent out an instant message over Skype to my launch team that said, "They're heeeeeeere and they want to buy!"

A few minutes later we went live right on time. The reaction was immediate. We were over $100,000 in sales in minutes, we hit $500,000 in the first hour, and when we closed down the launch a few days later we were over $3 million in sales.

Of course, not every launch will do $3 million dollars. In fact, I did dozens of launches before I got my first million-dollar launch. But even if the scale of your success isn't that big when you start out, the huge rush of momentum when you open your cart is just as big.

And frankly, I get more excited hearing about my students whose first launch did $3,000 or $8,000 or $27,000 than I do with the million-dollar launches. Hearing about those "smaller" launches when people are just starting out is a lot more exciting than hearing about the million-dollar launches by established companies, because I know once my students do that first launch, their lives are changed forever. They'll get to the bigger launches soon enough, but they'll never forget that moment when they pushed that send button and saw their first orders coming in.

Launch Day Nitty-Gritty

So first off, the term we generally use for launch day is "Open Cart" day, because that's the day you open your shopping cart and start taking orders. And as you might guess, the day your launch closes is called "Close Cart" day. Although you're often not technically closing your shopping cart on this day, you still need a clear end to your launch. But I'm getting ahead of myself. I'll get to that in a little bit.

So if you've followed my formula so far, you had a strong Prelaunch Sequence that led into your Open Cart. Your PLC connected with the people on your list. You hit the mental triggers to create a lot of authority, social proof, and community. And in the last few days of prelaunch you've started to hit on the scarcity trigger. Your list knows that you have an offer coming. Your final piece of PLC had a strong pivot where you started to foreshadow your offer. In other words, your prelaunch has already completed most of the heavy-lifting for you in terms of making the sale.

Now, the actual mechanics of opening your launch are pretty simple. You need to have a strong sales page. This is typically done through a sales video or a sales letter. And even though the people who have been through your Launch Sequence have already been pre-sold, it's important not to skimp on your sales message. You have to start with the opportunity, and then you need to tell the entire story of your offer.

Once you have your sales page ready, no matter whether you're using a sales video or a sales letter, the next step is simply a matter of sending an email to your launch list to let them know you're now live and open for business. This is a short, simple email with a link to your sales page. By now you've spent enough time and energy priming the pump, so you want this email to get right to the point.

Here's an example of an open cart email that I've used when I opened up my Product Launch Formula Coaching Program:

Okay, I just opened up registration for Product Launch Formula. We're now live:

CLICK HERE for Product Launch Formula
http://www.productlaunchformula.com

(I opened it up a bit early to avoid any bottlenecks and spread the load on the server.)

Best regards,
Jeff

P.S. Remember . . . you don't need to panic. I don't expect to sell out immediately. However, if you want one of those spots at my PLF Live Workshop, then please don't delay. They're going to go fast. Here's the link:

CLICK HERE for Product Launch Formula
http://www.productlaunchformula.com

As you can see, the email was short and simple. The open of the email had just one sentence before I gave the link to the sales letter. And, of course, when I sent this email, the link was clickable.

NOTE: The "PS" is often the single most read part of an email, and I used it to hit the scarcity trigger, warning my readers that they shouldn't delay or they risked missing out on my live workshop.

Before You Hit Send

At the risk of stating the obvious, before you send that open cart email, make sure you've gone through and tested—even retested— every step. Is your sales page live? Are all the links on the page working? Is your order form set up and proofread? Have you gone through the entire order process thoroughly? Do you know firsthand what happens after an order is placed? What about the thank you page after someone buys? The confirmation email? The fulfillment process?

If everything is tested and ready to go, it's time to send that email. And I have to tell you, no matter how many times I've done this, I get nervous every single time. I still hesitate before I hit that button to send the open cart email. It's a big moment, so expect to have some butterflies and feel some strong emotions. But once you've done your final checks, it's time. You are ready to launch.

Watching the Orders Roll In

Once your launch is live, the first hour or two often end up being something of a spectator sport. It's really, really hard not to obsess over the early results. You can breathe a sigh of relief when the first order comes in, because it means everything is working properly.

After that, I usually spend the next hour or two watching stats. I watch the traffic on the site, the traffic to the actual order form, the opens and clicks on the launch email, the number of orders, and the details behind the orders (which option people are choosing).

There's plenty of data, and you can make it a nearly full-time job to watch all of it. But after an hour or so, it's important to pull yourself away from the stats and get back to work, because your Open Cart has just begun.

(On my Resource Page I've got links to my favorite statistics and data tools. You can access that page at http://thelaunchbook.com/resources.)

Your Open Cart Strategy

So your open is certainly a big high point, but it's just a part of your entire Launch Sequence. Typically, you will want to keep your launch open somewhere between four to seven days. Sometimes my personal launches are shorter. There have been times I've completely sold out all of my product in as few as 24 or 36 hours.

But you should probably avoid doing a hyper-compressed launch like that until you've gone through a few launches and you have some experience. With a short-fuse launch, you have little time to recover if you make any mistakes. For your first launch, just plan on keeping your cart open for five days.

Your results will vary dramatically based on your market, your offer, and your entire launch strategy. However, typically you'll get about 25% of your orders in the first day and about 50% of your orders on the final day. The big first day is because you've built so much anticipation. The spike at the end of the launch is the scarcity trigger kicking in. Obviously, the rest of the orders will trickle in between your open and close.

The Big Close

One absolute, cardinal rule for creating a successful launch is setting a definitive close for your launch. And there must be some negative consequence if people don't buy during that limited open cart window. Make it clear that something bad will happen if they don't buy before your launch ends—that your prospects will miss out on something. That negative consequence is what creates scarcity, and it will generate a huge spike of sales in the last 24 hours of your launch.

IMPORTANT: Lots of people avoid creating real scarcity at the end of their launch. Don't make that mistake or you will cripple your results. In fact, you will cut your sales in half. Put some real teeth into the end of your launch, and you will double your results.

So what is that scarcity? What is that negative consequence if people don't jump onboard during your launch? There are three primary ways to create scarcity in your offer:

1. **The price goes up.** You have a special price during your launch, and people need to jump onboard during your launch to get that price. This is an easy one to understand. A "Grand Opening Sale" or Black Friday, the mega-shopping day after Thanksgiving in the U.S., are two familiar examples. While this is a good incentive to get people to jump during your launch and it's an easy one to use, it's not the most powerful form of scarcity during a launch.

2. **Remove bonuses.** Let's say you're selling a product that teaches people to play blues guitar. During your launch you have the special bonus of receiving a personal Skype guitar lesson from you. If they don't sign up

during your launch, then they don't get the bonus lesson. This can be a very powerful form of scarcity. If you have a strong bonus, this can actually be a stronger incentive than a price increase.

3. **The offer goes away.** If your prospects don't buy during the launch, then they get shut out of the opportunity—meaning, they can't take advantage of the offer at all, ever. In most cases, with most offers, this is the strongest form of scarcity—it's usually a much stronger incentive than the price going up. The only problem is that this type of scarcity doesn't fit well for a lot of offers. If you're opening a restaurant, then you don't want to close down after a week. I've personally used this form of scarcity quite a bit, especially with my online programs (like the Product Launch Formula Coaching Program). It makes a lot of sense for my offer, because I teach the program to groups of students in a similar fashion to a college class. That means registration is only available for a limited period of time when I'm starting a new class. If someone misses the registration period, then they can't get in. This type of scarcity is an extremely strong incentive for people to jump onboard if it fits with your product.

One key point: You can combine these three forms of scarcity and layer them on top of each other. If you can have the price go up and bonuses go away at the end of your launch, then you've just created more scarcity and a more powerful launch.

Finally, remember that using these types of scarcity are not about manipulation. The scarcity has to be real.

The reason this hard close for your launch works so well is that your prospects would much rather put off making a decision. And that goes double if the decision involves them opening their wallet and giving you money. If you have a great product that's going to make a big impact on their lives, then you owe it to your prospects to make the best offer possible to get them to overcome their procrastination. Ending your launch with an exclamation mark—meaning some form of scarcity that instills a sense of urgency—is the way you do that.

Beyond the Open and Close

It's critical that you don't let up during your open cart period. I've seen some of my students make this mistake, and they end up leaving a lot of money on the table. You need to keep mailing your launch list each day your cart is open. Here's how to use email to keep your launch in front of your prospects. For this example, we'll assume your launch lasts five days.

On launch day, you want to send out two emails—the first when you open the cart (see the email above) and the second about four hours later to let your list know that everything is up and running and you're open for business.

The day after your Open Cart, you should send one email—typically a social proof email, where you talk about the great response to your launch.

On Day Three you send a longer email that answers many of the top questions about the product. As with all your emails during your open cart period, you should include at least one link to your sales page.

On Day Four the message shifts to scarcity. You are basically giving a 24-hour warning ahead of your close. You should be absolutely clear about when you'll close and what your prospects stand to lose if they don't act before the launch offer closes down.

Then on Day Five you'll be mailing two (or even three) times. The first one is sent early in the morning reiterating that you're going to be closing that day. The second email goes out about six to eight hours before the cart closes. This is a day that will be filled with fireworks and a massive rush of orders—provided you follow this plan. Unfortunately, I've seen lots of people make the mistake of letting up on the last day. Either they don't mail their list at all or they just mail once. This typically happens when they start to worry that they've already sent too many emails during the launch and wonder what good one more email could do.

That's bad thinking. Don't make that mistake. You need to send more than one email on closing day. Trust me . . . doing so makes a big difference. Many of your prospects have a big procrastination streak, and they'll wait until the last minute. In fact, after you do your first launch and watch the final rush, I think you'll agree with me that MOST people are terrible procrastinators. It doesn't matter what time you close your launch, you will see people placing orders right up until the very last minute. So do yourself a favor—send at least two emails on your closing day, and consider sending a third.

When Stuff Goes Wrong

As much as I wish that everything always went perfectly and that every launch was a huge success, sometimes there are problems. Occasionally a launch can underperform. So I want to walk through some of the most common problems and give you a few pointers on what to do when your launch doesn't go well.

The first class of problems is technical. It's possible to crash your web site server if you send too much traffic. The good news is that this is not a problem you're likely to have with your first launch. It takes a huge launch with lots of traffic to cripple a server, and unless you've already got a significant business with a large list, you're probably not going to be putting a strain on your server.

However, if you do have a serious business with a large list, then this is definitely something to pay attention to. I crashed a server in one of my biggest launches, and it cost me a lot of heartache, plenty of orders, and ultimately a lot of money. It also cost me a lot of customer goodwill, and my reputation took a big hit. Make no mistake, server crashes are not fun. You can see my current list of recommended web hosts and servers on the Resource Page at http://thelaunchbook.com/resources.

Another problem that a lot of people don't think about is collecting the money—in other words, getting paid. If you're taking orders online, you're going to be using some type of payment gateway or merchant account. And no matter whom you're using, if you have a sudden huge influx of orders, it can make them nervous. Most likely they will look at that huge increase in orders as a credit risk and be worried that you might take all that money, not bother delivering your product, and then skip out to sit on a beach in Tahiti. And if you did something like that, they would be liable for all the refunds that would come pouring in. Bottom line, a huge increase in orders over your normal rate will scare your merchant account provider. I've personally run into this several times, both with my merchant accounts and with PayPal. The best way to avoid these troubles is through a lot of communication before your launch. And you should also do business with a "launch friendly" merchant account provider. There are providers that will understand when you tell them you're doing a "Jeff Walker-style launch." For a current list of my recommended providers, check out the Resource Page at http://thelaunchbook.com/resources.

What If No One Buys?

So what if your launch just doesn't convert? You open the cart and you have very few sales. As much as I would like to tell you that this doesn't ever happen, sometimes it does. When it does happen, it's time to go into diagnosis mode.

First off, if you have no sales at all, you need to start testing your process. Start with your launch email. Open up the email broadcast in your email program and try clicking through to the link to make sure it works. Then go through the sales process at your site and make sure everything is working. Does the sales page or sales letter load? Can you get to the order form? Try to place an order to make sure it goes through. Does everything work?

Next step is to determine whether you're getting any traffic to your site. Check the stats on your email broadcast. Did the email go out? Look at your stats. Did anyone click through to your site? What are the traffic stats on your web site telling you? How much traffic do you have to your sales page? To your order page?

Finally, if everything is working on the site and you're getting traffic to the site and you're still not getting any sales, then you've got a conversion problem. And in general, there are two primary reasons for conversion problems: It's either your offer or your sales message. It can be tough to tease out which of these are causing your low conversion, and it could possibly be a combination of both.

First let's look at the offer. Is your offer compelling? Does it offer a solution or solve a problem that your market cares about? Are you selling something that the market desperately wants as opposed to something you think they need or something that you just wanted to create? Does the offer address your prospects' hopes and dreams? Does it address the fears and aspirations in the market? Is it on point to what the market wants?

Now let's consider the sales message in your sales video or sales letter. Does your sales message articulate the transformation or the change your product offers to your prospect? Does it make the benefits in your product come alive? Does it make those benefits feel tangible and concrete? Is your buying process simple and understandable or is it confusing in any way? Do you clearly tell your prospects exactly what they're going to get? What they can expect with every step of the process? How much the product costs? What your guarantee is?

If you determine that you have either an offer problem or a sales copy problem, then it's time to get to work. It's not too late to pull a rabbit out of the hat. I've seen remarkable turnarounds right in the middle of the launch due to a tweaked offer and/or a reworked sales page.

Keep the Good Times Rolling—What to Do after Your Launch

One of the most powerful and surprising results of doing these launches is the amount of goodwill that you will create. When you deliver real value in your Prelaunch Content, your market will fall in love with you . . . both the people who buy from you AND the people who just watch your Prelaunch Content but don't buy.

Not everyone will love you, of course, but a big chunk of the market will. Those people are your tribe, and your prelaunch creates a great self-selection process for identifying that tribe.

Once you've gone through your launch and closed your cart, you will want to strengthen your relationship with those who bought from you. This is the "post launch," and it's critical that you use it to extend your momentum and positioning from your launch. I make a huge effort to over-deliver to my new clients, and I suggest you do the same. I always have a few extra bonuses that I never mentioned during my launch, and I start sending out those bonuses shortly after the cart closes. In these days where we are so often underwhelmed by our experience after we buy a product, adding something extra makes you stand out in the market. It's amazing what a few extra unannounced bonuses will do. You don't have to go crazy . . . just give more than you promised.

One of the biggest—and easiest—wins you will have in your market comes from putting together a solid new-client, follow-up process. And much of this can be done through automated follow-up emails.

Another area you shouldn't skimp on is customer service. I provide world-class customer service, and it's worth every penny I spend on it. I don't look at customer service as a cost center, but as a big part of my overall strategic business building.

Finally, don't forget about following up with the prospects who did NOT buy. You just spent considerable energy romancing them in your prelaunch, and even if they didn't buy this time, they are still great prospects for future offers. Don't let that romance go cold. Send them some more content in the days after you close your launch. Then they'll be primed for a follow-up offer or for your next launch.

So now that we've gone through the launch, I've got something special in store for you—the secrets of the Seed Launch™, which is all about how to do a launch even if you don't have a list or a product. And I'll show you how I built up a business from a simple Seed Launch right into a $20+ million empire . . .

How to Start from Scratch: The Seed Launch™

Chapter 9

T ara and Dave Marino's lives were turned upside down by the loss of their young child. It's a nightmare that no parent wants to even think about. I can't imagine that pain, but I do know the pain of losing someone who is very close and who passes way before their time. It's not easy to move beyond that type of loss.

Dave had a great, secure job that paid him more than six figures, year in and year out, but he felt like he was drifting in corporate cubicle-land. And after the tragic loss of his child, he found it difficult to get excited about anything in his life. Tara sold a little real estate on the side, but she was mostly a stay-at-home mom with two young kids.

Tara, however, had a passion—helping her friends, mostly other moms and wives like herself, live a more sensual life. When she first heard about the Product Launch Formula, she knew it was exactly the right tool to bring her message to a bigger audience and build her business. And she thought it might even give Dave something that would spark a new outlook on life.

But Tara faced a huge challenge—she was starting from scratch. After helping her friends, she knew she had the raw material for a program about leading a more sensual life, but she didn't have a book or a seminar or even a speech. And she certainly didn't have a product.

Another problem: She didn't have any type of an email list or any platform whatsoever. She had a few followers on Twitter and some Facebook friends, but that was about it.

So given a situation like Tara's, how do you get started?

Getting Paid before You Create Your Product

With the magic of the Seed Launch™, you can literally create a business from almost nothing . . . which is exactly what Tara did.

She pulled together a list of about 200 people from her personal inbox and social media, and she started her prelaunch. The product would be called "You're Perfect." To hear Tara and Dave talk about it now, the whole venture was a rag-tag process they made up on the fly. But when you're launching your first product to a tiny list like they had, you can often overcome any mistakes due to your close connection with the people on your list. And in her Seed Launch, Tara was able to sell five spots in her training program and make almost $3,000 in sales!

The product was a series of six weekly teleseminars, along with worksheets and templates. That meant Tara was creating and delivering the product after she already had made the sale. Each week she created the material for the call, then she got on the phone and delivered a class. And since the entire process was extremely interactive, she was able to use the feedback from her clients to fine-tune the next call to exactly what they needed. Of course, Tara recorded each call, and those recordings became the basis for her product after the initial program was finished. The Seed Launch delivered a payday and a finished product.

Now making almost $3,000 from scratch is incredibly exciting, but it's what happened next that makes this an amazing story. Because as Tara delivered that first training class, all the interaction gave her the idea for two more products: "The Power of Sensuality" and "The Beauty Formula." And with the momentum from that first launch, Dave and Tara were able to build up a list of a thousand email subscribers. Their next launch did almost $12,000 in sales—a huge increase from their first launch. But again, that was just the beginning. The next promotion brought in $90,000, and then another did $190,000. Each launch built their list and their reputation in the market. They have now done over a half million dollars in sales of Tara's products, trainings, and coaching.

Along the way, Dave quit his job. Suddenly the "security" of cubicle-land didn't look all that great. And while no business success can ever take away their pain of losing their child, they've built an entirely new life for their family. That new life took a dramatic turn when Tara and Dave and their two young sons took a summer trip to France, and they decided to stay! Tara had always dreamed of living in France, and her new business and lifestyle suddenly made it possible . . . so they flew home, put most of their stuff in storage, and moved to the south of France.

(To read the full Case Study of Tara and Dave, go to http://thelaunchbook. com/tara.)

When You're Just Starting Out

At this point I'm sure you can see the power of a well-orchestrated product launch. And you've seen how Product Launch Formula has been the proven system that's worked over and over for businesses of any size.

But I've been at this long enough to know there are some folks who just don't see how it can work for them, especially if they're just starting out. You might be one of those people. Perhaps you're thinking that while this all makes sense, you don't know how to get started. You don't have a list of prospects or you don't have a product to sell. Maybe you're thinking how you would love to launch something, but you have neither a product nor a list. Or maybe you've got a business right now, but you would like to start a different business. You're ready to move on, but you don't know where to start. Well, this is the chapter for you, because the Seed Launch provides the answers to all these questions.

I call it the Seed Launch because it's a little launch that can grow a product, a list, and even a business into a great big success. Think of a tiny seed that can one day become a towering oak tree that stands a hundred feet tall. To look at that seed and think it can grow to such an incredible size seems improbable at best, yet we know that's exactly what happens. And it's no different with a Seed Launch. It starts with an idea and a handful of sales, but it can grow into a serious business.

Disaster Strikes One Sunny Friday Afternoon

Before I get into the exact mechanics of a Seed Launch, let me give you an example that shows just how it can work and how far-reaching the impact can be. This Seed Launch took place in 2005, and like many launches it was driven by a serious need. In fact, this was my launch, and I was starting over from scratch.

After a number of years in business with a variety of products and services, I had a partnership break apart very abruptly. I've had many partnerships over the years, and the one thing you learn about partnerships is that, by their very definition, none of them can last forever. In any case, this partnership ended without warning. One Friday afternoon my partner called me to say not only was he leaving the partnership, he would be taking almost all of our paying clients with him.

Most business people have been through something similar to this. As I say, the situation is not all that unusual. But it sure has a way of focusing your attention. So the first thing I did was sit down and think about what type of business I wanted to create next. I spent a lot of time listing what I liked and what I didn't like about the business that had just disappeared. And then I created a criteria list of the changes I would want in my new business. And spent a lot of time selecting the niche I wanted to target with this new business. And most important, I focused on what value I could bring to the market.

For years, I had focused on the investing and trading niche. All my products had been about teaching people how to invest in the stock market. Although I loved that business, I was burned out. I had been publishing my stock market newsletters an average of more than five hundred times per year. And since I did it all without any staff, the whole process had become a real grind. I was ready to move onto a different market that had a lot fewer deadlines.

And there was another driving factor to consider: I had recently discovered a passion for entrepreneurship and marketing. I knew nothing of marketing when I first started out, but over the years I had developed a real knack for it. I had created my first business out of nothing, built a huge list of subscribers, and invented this crazy system for launching my products. In fact, I had been sharing my product launch techniques with some other entrepreneurs, and they had been getting outstanding results, so I knew my method would work for others just as well as they worked for me.

So I had an area of expertise (marketing and product launches) that could create a lot of value for people, and I loved the entire niche of entrepreneurship and marketing. But I had two problems: I had neither a list nor a product in that market. The big email lists from my previous business were made up of people who were interested in the stock market; those lists wouldn't do me any good in this new venture. But I did have one thing going for me—I had been invited to speak at a marketing conference that would take place in just a few weeks. I decided I would use my talk at that conference to begin building my new business.

I put together a great presentation that walked through my entire launch process—or at least as much as I could fit into a 90-minute presentation. Then at the end of the presentation I made an offer: If anyone in the audience wanted to go deeper and learn exactly how to implement my strategies, I would coach a small group of clients through every step of the process. I called it the "Product Launch Workshop." The coaching would take place via a series of teleclasses that I would be conducting after the event.

There is an art form to "selling from the stage," and let me just say I was neither skilled nor experienced at this practice. So my offer at the end of the talk did not get an overwhelming response. There were nearly three hundred people in attendance, and I sold only six spots in my workshop. That's not a very strong performance. I now know that a 10% response rate is at the lower end of what you should expect after you make an offer from stage, and I had gotten less than 3%.

Nevertheless, I realized that while I might not be a great pitchman, I definitely knew how to do product launches. And I now had real, live clients. I was confident that I could give them a skill that would forever change their lives.

A Couple of Problems . . . Solved!

At that point I had a couple of other problems. First, I knew how to do launches, but I didn't necessarily know how to teach them. And second, to get a strong level of participation, I wanted more than six people in the class. So I invited several of my entrepreneurial friends, other business owners I had met over the years, to join the class. Since I understood that it was far more important to get a "critical mass" in the class than to extract every last dollar out of it, I extended the invitation on a complimentary basis. Many of these people knew of my successful launches, and they were eager to learn my formula . . . so this was a win-win for them. I got my critical mass, and they got to learn my secrets. And that brought the total class size up to just over 30 people.

So that solved my critical mass problem, but I still had the problem of figuring out the best way to teach the material. I knew how to do launches, but I hadn't taught my formula before. And I knew from experience that when you're an expert on a topic, you often suffer from "the curse of knowledge." You forget what it's like to be a beginner, and you end up teaching at too high a level.

So I went back to one of my favorite tools—the one I taught you when we covered the pre-prelaunch. I asked my audience what they wanted to know. As part of my offer, I promised five teleclasses. But before I did even the first one, I surveyed my 30 students to learn their most burning questions about product launches. I took the responses and split them into five broad categories to correspond with the five calls I would make. For the first call, I took all the questions for that specific topic, which was a broad overview of the product launch process, and put them in a logical sequence. Then I simply went through and answered each question on the call.

Before the next call, I ran another survey. I asked my students if they had any questions about the material I covered in the first call. And then I asked them for their top questions about the second topic—creating the Prelaunch Sequence. Once again, I arranged those questions in a compelling sequence and went through all the questions on the teleclass.

I continued that process for each call—wash, rinse, repeat. After I had completed all five teleclasses, I added an extra bonus call where I answered any additional questions my students had. And then, because I've always been obsessed with over-delivering on my promises, I added a few extra Case Study calls where I walked through examples from some additional launches.

In the end, I think I ended up doing nine or ten calls instead of the five I had promised. We went deep, and I taught everything I knew. And that led to some terrific testimonials and several successful Case Studies from my students. Those testimonials were partly because I had over-delivered and partly because my material (which later became Product Launch Formula) was truly revolutionary. But there was also a third very important reason my students loved the course so much, and it's critical that you understand this third reason.

Simply put, even though I had never taught the material before, I did a great job teaching it. And the reason why wasn't because I'm a natural-born teacher. It was because I let my students guide the process. I continually asked them, both on the calls and in the surveys before each call, what they needed to know. What wasn't clear in the material I delivered? What did I need to go back and cover more thoroughly? What unanswered questions did they have? In effect, I used that first group of students from my Seed Launch to learn how to teach the material.

In my current position in the industry, I get to see a lot of products come to market. And many of them are not very good. Using the Seed Launch removes the worry that you're going to create a lousy product. It gives you an interactive process to build your product, and when you involve your clients by asking for their input you end up with a great product. Simply put, you naturally become attuned to your market's need. There is no guesswork. You avoid the curse of knowledge. And you deliver true value to your clients.

Your Seed Launch

So let's get to the nitty-gritty of the Seed Launch.

This is the ideal launch if you're just starting out and you don't have a list or a product. It's also great if you have an idea for a new product, but you aren't sure of the demand for it or you would like to get paid for a product before you create it. What you're going to find is that the Seed Launch is enormously flexible. The one real limitation is that this style of launch doesn't work for physical widgets. But if you have a knowledge- or learning-based product, then this is a perfect fit. If you want to teach how to lose weight, build a better relationship, find a better job, run your first marathon, train your dog, bring in more chiropractic patients, get more followers in social media . . . or anything like that, then you're going to love the Seed Launch.

The good news is that by now we've already learned nearly all the tools and concepts that you need in your Seed Launch. The even better news is that the Seed Launch is the simplest launch of all. And the best news is that you're going to end up with your own product by the time you wrap it up, and it's going to be a great product that's perfectly tuned to your prospects' needs and desires.

The Seed Launch takes advantage of two phenomena that very few people are aware of unless they've done some list-based direct marketing. The first is that, on a percentage basis, smaller lists are more responsive than bigger lists. And I'm not talking a LITTLE more responsive—I mean they're a LOT more responsive. For instance, I once did a launch to a list of 299 people. I was trying to make one of the most difficult sales ever by taking an online service that had originally been free and charging for that exact same service. And the new price was not inexpensive, but $100 per year.

On the face of it, I was looking at an extremely difficult sale. But the list was very warm (in other words, I had a very strong relationship with the people on the list). In the end, I had 297 out of the 299 sign up for the product, which gave me a conversion rate of 99.3%. That's one conversion stat that I'm pretty sure I'll never be able to top! (And my results were certainly not typical!) But more to the point, if the list was three thousand people, then I wouldn't have had anywhere near that conversion rate.

The second little-known leverage point the Seed Launch capitalizes on is that in every list there's a percentage of people known as "hyper-responsives." These are your raving fans. They open up every email or letter you send them. They'll eagerly buy whatever you offer. These people are the first you hear from every time you send an email, the first to comment on your blog, the first to pass along your social media updates. The good news is—these hyper-responsives exist in nearly every list.

And when you combine the fact that small lists are more responsive and there are hyper-responsives lurking in that small list, you have the seeds of . . . well . . . a Seed Launch.

Of course, you might be wondering why I'm telling you all about small lists when I said you could do a Seed Launch with no list. Well, the first step in your Seed Launch is to build some type of micro-list. That list might have only 30 people, but it would be better if it contained more like a hundred people. And three hundred would be even better.

But the good news is that pulling together a micro-list like this has never been easier, and your most-effective tool is social media. The process of getting those first subscribers is as simple as starting to post good content about your topic on social media sites like Facebook, Twitter, and whatever new darling emerges in the social media world.

Since social media moves faster than books can be published, and since the Seed Launch will still be working decades after I write these words, I'm not going to give you exact tactics on how to build a micro-list via social media. But at the end of the day, you attract followers by publishing relevant interesting content about your topic. It can either be content you create or content you curate (i.e., stuff from others that you find and repost). Either way, it doesn't take long to attract a small following. Again, aim for one hundred to three hundred. It's really not very hard.

The entire goal of the Seed Launch is not to make a million dollars but to get you in the game, help you automatically create a great product and learn about your market, and set you up for a bigger launch just a bit further down the road.

So just like I did with my Seed Launch of the Product Launch Workshop, your offer is going to be a series of teleseminars. That means you and all your clients call into a "bridge line." This is a simple phone call you make into a special number. The bridge line is set up so that everyone else can hear you—sort of like a conference call. Essentially, you can give a lecture over the phone to your students. If you want, you have the control to unmute the lines so your students can speak on the call. I've done teleseminars where I presented to thousands of people, but when you're delivering your product after your Seed Launch, you'll probably have only a few dozen people on your calls.

A quick note: You could choose to do webinars instead of teleseminars. On a webinar, your students will be able to see your computer screen in addition to hearing you speak. Webinars can be great because they give you the capability to teach visually, but they're also slightly more complicated to deliver. You could even do a series of live, in-person trainings if your audience is local. But the easiest way to start is with teleseminars. You can get more details on bridge lines and teleseminar services on the Resource Page at http://thelaunchbook.com/resources.

So let's just say you're going to do a series of three teleseminars about your topic. (Again, you could do any number that makes sense, but most of the time three to five calls works best.) Plan on doing one per week. Also plan on doing a surprise bonus "Question and Answer" call just to make sure that you over-deliver to your new clients.

About the actual launch . . . since you're going to be selling to a small, warm list that almost certainly has a number of hyper-responsives, your launch doesn't need to be elaborate. Just use what I taught you in Chapters 6 and 7.

But you do need to have a good offer, and you need to do a good job of explaining the benefits people will receive from your class. That means you focus on the transformation or change people will experience by going through your training. You must show your clients how you're going to help them reach their dreams and aspirations and/or avoid their fears and frustrations. So, for example, if you're going to teach someone how to play guitar, don't focus on how quickly they will learn to switch between all the primary open chords; instead, focus on the transformation they will go through. What will the final outcome be? Will they finally be able to play songs for themselves and their friends? Will they gain the confidence to start playing with other people? Will they finally feel like a real musician? Will they get more dates?

So let's get to your launch. With the Seed Launch you want to keep things simple, beginning with the pre-prelaunch. In fact, your pre-pre will do a lot of the heavy lifting for your launch. Go back and review the pre-prelaunch chapter, then run a classic pre-pre "ask" campaign where you ask your micro-list to tell you their most burning questions. You can do this either by putting together an actual survey or via email or social media. That survey will tell you a lot about the hopes/dreams/fears/frustrations of your market . . . and it will be invaluable as you put together your offer. And, of course, your pre-pre is a shot-across-the-bow—it sets the stage for your offer and starts to build awareness and even anticipation of your coming offer.

After the initial survey in your pre-prelaunch, your next step is an email follow up, where you talk about some of the findings and conclusions from your survey. You can share some of your own journey of transformation, such as some of your early challenges and how you overcame them. And at the end of your email, you can talk a little bit about your upcoming class.

After that, your next email is where you make your offer. Generally, you will want to direct people to a sales letter or sales video. But remember, you don't need to oversell. The people on your micro-list will feel like they have a personal relationship with you (and for many of them that will likely be true). So you want your sales message to reflect that. Of course, you still have to work hard to explain the benefits, and you still need to focus on the ultimate transformation or change that your new clients will experience. But you don't want to come across as a used-car salesman, because that won't resonate with your micro-list.

Your goal in all of this is to get 30 people (60 would be even better) to say yes and buy your product. You want that many people because you want to have a lot of interaction. And attrition is a sad fact of human nature . . . you'll almost always have some people who just don't show up or participate in any way. So if you start with 30 people, then you'll still have some sticking around at the end. If you don't sell 30 spots, do what I did with my Product Launch Workshop and discreetly invite a few people to participate on a complimentary basis. And if you come up short of 30, that's okay. Tara started with five, and I started with six.

A quick note on prices and sales: I've seen Seed Launches for products between $50 and $3,000 (depending on the market and offer), so your financial results are going to vary dramatically from person to person and from offer to offer. But remember, this is more about building a great product and getting you in the game than it is about the money.

Now, as you deliver your product, remember that feedback and surveys are your friend. I survey people before each call. I ask them what their top questions about the next topic are. So back to that "learn guitar" example. If the first call is about "how to strum the guitar," I would briefly explain the topic in one sentence, then ask, "What are your top two questions about strumming the guitar?"

Your job isn't to get on the phone and answer every question. You want to go through the responses, group them into themes, and rewrite them into good questions that you can expand into teaching points. Then put them in a logical and compelling order. Once you've done that, you're ready to get on the phone and give a great presentation.

After that first call, you send out another survey. First you ask if there are any additional questions about the topic of the first call (e.g., "How to Strum Your Guitar"). Then you ask for the top questions on your next topic. Repeat this process before and after every call. The happy result is that you're building a product to perfectly match what your market wants. And along the way, you're getting deep insight into your market and how to talk to your market . . . and that's going to pay off in a big way when it comes time for you to do your first big launch. It might seem almost criminal, but you're getting paid to gather all this market research.

Of course, you're going to be recording these calls—something most bridge lines will do for you automatically. If you do five calls, and then add in your bonus Q&A call, you've now created six audio recordings. And you can get those audio recordings transcribed. Each hour of audio will equal about 15 to 20 printed pages, so you'll have the makings of a book (or ebook) that's 90 to 120 pages long. Now you've got audio and a book and there's your multimedia product. BOOM! You just got paid to create a product!

You will also want to focus on getting your new clients some strong results, because they're going to be great candidates for Case Studies as you move forward and get ready to launch your product in a bigger way.

So that's the essence of the Seed Launch—simple, fast, flexible. And it sets the stage for much bigger launches to come in your business. It's the perfect way to dip your toe in the water, learn how to teach your topic, learn about the hopes, dreams, and fears of your target market, and create a great product without much effort.

From Seed Launch to Empire

And just to show you where a Seed Launch can go, there's a postscript to the story of my Product Launch Workshop Seed Launch. Even though I was able to convince only six people to buy my Product Launch Workshop, I felt like I had a winner on my hands. The people who went through the training loved it. And once they started to put my teachings to work in their businesses, the results started to roll in. It was the beginning of the huge tide of Product Launch Formula success stories from nearly every market and niche you could imagine.

Now, being the perfectionist that I am, I took all the material I had delivered in that first workshop, and I re-created it in a more polished version. I used all the lessons I had learned about teaching the material, and I added in some of my students' Case Studies. A few months later I finished the creation of the first ever Product Launch Formula course.

And, of course, I had to put together a product launch for it. That was October, 2005. In the one-week launch that followed I did more than $600,000 in sales. Since that time I've done over $20 million in sales of PLF, and I now have over ten thousand PLF Owners. And you're part of this story as well, because you would not be holding this book in your hand if it weren't for that first very modest Seed Launch that I did. That just shows what can happen when you start with a Seed Launch and continue to leverage up your launches.

One thing to remember about those numbers: Even though I had previously run a successful business, I was starting over again. I had entered a completely new market with a completely new product. The big list I had from my prior business was of no use to me. I was starting from scratch again, and the Seed Launch is how I started out.

However, I had one more "secret weapon" in my arsenal to help build my new business, and that weapon let me come out of the gate with that $600,000 launch—the biggest launch I had ever done. So how did I do it in a brand-new market? In a market where I had no presence and almost no list?

My secret was the enormous power of the "JV Launch," and that's what the next chapter is all about . . .

How I Made a Million Dollars in a Single Hour: The JV Launch

Chapter 10

S o exactly where is the line between fear and panic?

The minutes were counting down toward the open cart time much too quickly, and I was far too stressed and sleep-deprived. It had been more than 48 hours since I had gotten anything more substantial than a catnap. I was getting bombarded with emails and instant messages with questions, comments, suggestions. The traffic to my site was like nothing I had ever experienced. This wasn't my first rodeo—I had already done dozens of launches. But the stakes were a lot higher this time, and I was playing on a much bigger stage.

The clock was ticking down, and I still had lots to do. I needed a headline. I needed to test the order process. I needed to mail my list. I needed to communicate with my partners. Arrrrrgggghhhh . . . The minutes kept ticking away toward the open at 10AM Mountain Standard Time.

It had been a little more than six months since my prior business had imploded due to a partnership breakup, and it was time for a "revenue event"— meaning time to make some money. I was ready to be back in business. But this time I wanted a business where I had complete control, where I didn't have a partner to consult every time I had a new idea or plan.

And I was ready to leave the stock market niche behind. I had loved the stock market when I started that business, but I had come to realize that I loved marketing even more, and I was really good at it. I knew I didn't want to be a marketing consultant. After years of being an information entrepreneur, I was in love with publishing and teaching. I was in love with the inherently leveraged nature of the business; my income wasn't tied to the number of hours I worked but to how well I could sell my products. And I was also in love with the impact I could make. Instead of helping a few dozen people as a consultant, I could impact thousands as a publisher. And I was clearly legit—I'd been making a living with a marketing-driven business on the Internet for longer than most people had access to the Internet.

I had only one issue. It was a crowded market. There were thousands of people who were trying to make a living as an Internet marketing expert. Some of them were wildly successful, but the majority of them could barely afford their business cards. And it was a market in which I had no positioning or traction. Even though I had long been doing business online, even though I had a completely revolutionary new way to sell online, even though I had been making more money online than most of the so-called Internet marketing gurus . . . well, none of that mattered because I didn't have a presence in the niche. All my email lists and web sites were about the stock market. My tens of thousands of email subscribers in the stock market niche wouldn't do me any good starting a business in the Internet marketing niche.

However, I did have an ace in the hole. It was only one card, but it was a powerful one, and I was going to play that card with everything I had.

A couple years earlier, in February 2003, I had attended an Internet marketing seminar. When I walked into that seminar, I felt like I had found my tribe.

Doing business online back in those days could be lonely. I fought the good fight every day out of my home office, but almost no one understood what I was doing. The idea of an online business was completely foreign to almost everyone.

But at that seminar, I was suddenly among a couple of hundred other people who did the same thing I did—they all had the same hopes, dreams, challenges, and frustrations. And at the back of that conference room a small group of us forged a bond that would last for years and change an entire industry. But that was all in the distant future.

In the short term, I learned one important fact—that the product launches I had quietly been doing in my stock market business were truly unique. No one else was doing anything like them. Before that seminar, I didn't realize how unusual my product launches were. I had recently done the launch that brought in $106,000 in seven days and helped me buy my house. But I didn't realize just how unusual that result was, and I didn't realize how unusual my strategies were. I had assumed that I couldn't be the only person doing these types of launches. I had figured it out on my own, so I assumed others must have done the same. But I was wrong. Each time I mentioned one of the launches I had done in my business, everyone listening would go silent and their ears would perk up. My launches seemed to defy the normal laws of marketing and business.

I left that seminar with lots of new friendships—some of them with people who were leaders in the Internet marketing industry. These were people with lists and connections. At that time I was still publishing about the stock market and years away from thinking about publishing in the Internet marketing niche. But I loved talking to my new friends because of our shared passion for marketing and business-building. At some point, I started helping a few of them put together product launches, and they enjoyed some spectacular successes with those launches. Word slowly filtered throughout many of the major players in the nascent Internet marketing industry that this guy Jeff Walker had a brand-new technique that could bring in crazy profits in a very short period of time. I didn't know it at the time, but I was sowing the seeds for my next business.

My First JV Launch

One of the critical components of any launch is your list of prospects. As I showed you in the Seed Launch chapter, it's entirely possible to do a smaller-scale launch when you're first starting out without a list (or with just a tiny micro-list). But if you're going to make a big impression in the market, you need a list. Now there are lots of ways to build a list, but the single fastest way to do it is by using the lists that other people have already built and curated. That's the essence of a Joint Venture Launch (also known as a JV Launch).

In a JV Launch you have partners mail their lists and tell their people about your launch. If you make a sale to one of the people your partner sends your way, you pay your partner a commission.

The way this generally works is that your JV partners will mail their list and encourage their readers to visit your Prelaunch Content. In most JV Launches, the JV partners actually send their list to your squeeze page, so that the visitors have to join your list before they get to your PLC. Throughout your launch, you follow up with your new prospects. You use special affiliate tracking software (see the Resource Page at http://thelaunchbook.com/resources) on your web site to track which JV partner referred each prospect. Then when you Open Cart and start making sales, your software automatically tracks who referred each new client to you so you can pay commissions to the right partner.

One of the most powerful byproducts of doing a JV Launch like this is that you end up building a serious "launch list" out of all those leads. And after you do the launch, you get to keep that list. This is the single fastest way there is to grow a list. Of course, list size is completely dependent on your niche, who your partners are, and the size of their list, but it's possible to add thousands of people to your list in just a few days during a JV Launch.

And that's exactly what happened to me. Because I had built relationships with the leaders in the Internet marketing industry—and often gave them lots of help with their launches—these experts were ready and willing to help me out. So when I came out with my first piece of Prelaunch Content, I had many of the major players on board and mailing their lists about my PLC. Within a couple of days, I had 8,000 people join my list. And it didn't stop there. My JV partners kept mailing throughout my prelaunch, and I built a list of more than 15,000 email subscribers during the launch. That was a breathtaking number. In my old stock market business, where I was operating in a much bigger niche, it took me years to build a list that size. And now I had done it in a matter of days in my new business—all through the power of my JV partners.

And there I was on October 21, 2005, just a few minutes before it was time to Open Cart on my launch, and yes . . . I was scared. And there was an important reason for that fear.

It wasn't that I doubted my capabilities. I knew I could put together a great launch, and I knew I had a great product. And the feedback I had gotten during the prelaunch told me that everything about my offer was resonating with my prospects. So it was clear that my launch was hitting on all cylinders.

But since it was a JV Launch, I felt an extra layer of responsibility. My partners had trusted me with their support, and it was my job to make that trust pay off. I'll cover this in more detail a little later, but you have to treat your JV relationships like gold. And that's why I was extra nervous as the minutes ticked away before my open.

Of course, if my partners had any doubt about the result, they were blown away in the opening minutes of the launch. Within the first hour, I had already done more than $70,000 in sales. By the end of the first day, after only 14 hours, the sales were over $200,000. When I closed down the launch a week later, the final sales total was just over $600,000. Not a bad way to start a new business—especially since it was in a brand new market, with a brand new product, and I had spent zero dollars on advertising. And I did all this from my home office out in the mountains of Colorado, and my only staff was my wife, Mary, helping me with customer service. No, not a bad way to start a new business.

Of course, the devil is always in the details, and as is true with any business venture I certainly had costs. All those sales didn't flow directly into my wallet. One of the biggest costs in a JV Launch is your affiliate commissions. Your JV partners are not going to mail their lists about your launch out of the goodness of their heart. The core part of the JV Launch, which makes it work for everyone, is that you track who the leads and sales came from, and you pay commissions on the sales you make to those leads. In this case, I was paying 50% of the sale to my referring partner. Back with that very first launch of Product Launch Formula, the price was $997, so I paid a commission of $498.50 for every sale that a partner referred to me.

I often have students ask me what's a typical commission to pay JV partners. My answer is always the same: There is no "typical." A commission varies by launch, by market, by niche, and even by partner. What you pay, and exactly how you structure your JV compensation, is a business decision. I was able to pay a 50% commission because the margin on my product is relatively large. In my business, the costs are all involved with actually generating the lead and making the sale. But other businesses will be different. If you're selling physical goods (computers, barbeque grills, humidors, etc.), then the commissions you pay are going to be a lot lower. There are even some markets where the initial commissions are a lot higher than 50%. Such can be the case where there is a lot more revenue in the "back end" sales—that is, the follow-up sales after the original sale.

No matter how you structure your JV compensation, one big advantage of this type of promotion is that you pay your commission AFTER the sale is made. Compare that to standard advertising, where you spend a bunch of money before you even know if the advertising is going to work. No matter if it's TV, radio, newspaper, online, direct mail, yellow pages, or some other medium, your money is spent and you're left hoping to get a return on that upfront investment. With JV or affiliate relationships, you pay based only on the results, and you pay after the sale is made.

Affiliate or JV Partner: What's the Difference?

So exactly what is the difference between a JV partner and an affiliate? They're actually pretty much the same. In each case, you're talking about someone who is going to promote your product and get paid a commission if one of the prospects they refer to you buys something. So if Affiliate John sends Prospect Alice to your web site to look at your product, and Prospect Alice buys your product, then you'll pay Affiliate John a commission. You set the level of the commission (as either a percentage of the sale or a fixed dollar amount per sale), and that commission level is part of your agreement with Affiliate John.

The mechanics of this arrangement are the same whether we're talking about JV partners or affiliates, and you can really use the terms interchangeably. However, the terms "JV" or "JV partner" generally imply a closer relationship. I know almost all of my JV partners personally, and during a launch I'm communicating with them closely— always via email and often on the phone or via text. Many of them are close friends of mine.

Why JV Launches Work When you look at all the advantages of a JV Launch (far bigger sales, crazy fast list building, huge positioning in your market), this might sound like the answer to everyone's problems. However, there are some core elements you need to have in place before you even think about a JV Launch, and there are many mistakes to be avoided. So let's walk through this one step at a time.

The first thing you have to remember is that, just like you, your potential JV partners are in business to make a profit. If they've built up a substantial, responsive list, that is a considerable asset they've put a lot of time and investment into. The odds are very high that they understand just how powerful an asset their list is, and they're not going to be interested in mailing their list about any old launch that comes wandering down the lane. In other words, just because you put together a Launch Sequence and an offer, don't expect them to be falling all over themselves to promote your launch. The fact is, if they have a strong list they probably have more opportunities to promote offers than they can possibly accommodate. That's reality. (And if they don't have a strong list, they're not going to be a very good partner, so you shouldn't be bothering with them.) A list can be mailed to only so many times, and anyone with a substantial list most likely gets requests every day to promote someone else's product. To have a good list is to possess a scarce resource.

This is where a well-constructed Launch Sequence shines. Since a Launch Sequence is such an incredible conversion machine, you're going to be generating some outsized results. And that generally means outsized commissions for your JV partners. One of the ways this is measured online is in EPC—or "earnings per click"—which is the amount of commissions someone gets for everyone who clicks through to a promotion. So if someone sends 100 clicks, and those clicks generate commissions of $450 for the partner, then that's an EPC of 450/100, or a $4.50 EPC.

I often get the question "What's a good EPC?" There is no single answer to that question because an EPC will vary depending on the market and offer. What's important is that if your launch can generate a strong EPC relative to the other offers in your market, then it's going to be a lot easier to convince partners to mail for you. And again, a solid PLF-style launch is an EPC-generating monster.

Don't Test with Your Partners' Lists

If you're going to have any success in the JV game, you need to build long-term relationships with your partners. I see plenty of people approaching this like a "one and done" type of relationship, but that makes it really tough to have any type of longevity in your business.

The reality is that when your partners promote your offer, they're going to be watching their numbers, meaning they're going to be watching their EPC. And they're also going to be watching what type of experience you provide for the people they referred to you, because that experience will reflect on them. If they tell the people on their list to go watch your videos, and your videos are boring and content-free, it will negatively impact what those visitors think about your partner. So your partner has real skin in the game. Mailing for your launch has real costs and substantial risks to your partner. And if the results from their promotion aren't good, then they probably won't be promoting for you again in the future. Before you ask someone to mail for you, you need to be sure you have an offer that converts.

Fortunately, there's an easy way to make sure your launch will perform for your partner, and that's to do an Internal Launch first. In other words, first run the launch for just your list (even if you have a very small list). That way you get to test your Launch Sequences and your offer. That's how you can be sure you have a winner before you ask your JV partners to take a chance on promoting your offer to their list.

When I tell my students to do an Internal Launch first, many of them want to skip over that little bit of coaching. They want to jump directly to the excitement and glory (and big dollars) of the JV Launch. There are several reasons to avoid doing that. When you do an Internal Launch, it gives you the opportunity to test out all your systems and get some experience under your belt. That's really important, but what's truly critical is that you have the opportunity to test your offer and your Prelaunch Sequence to make sure you've got a winner. This is the deal—you never want to test an offer with a partner's list. You don't want your partners being your guinea pig. If you have an offer that isn't going to convert, you want to be the one taking that bullet.

Remember, your relationships with your JV partners should be treated like gold. You need to nurture and cherish them so they turn into long-term relationships. I said this above, but it's so critical that it bears repeating: If you ask a JV partner to mail an offer and it doesn't convert, then there's a good chance they're not going to mail for your next offer. On the other hand, if you've got a tested and proven offer (i.e., an offer that you ran an Internal Launch for), and you can show them your results, then they're going to be a lot more interested in mailing. And they're going to be a lot more likely to get some great results. And the better their results, the more likely they'll mail for you in the future.

Getting JV Partners

It's obvious that the JV Launch has some really huge benefits, so how do you go about getting great JV partners? This is a big topic, and I've spent entire days teaching about finding and nurturing JV relationships. But I'm going to do my best to break it down for you in a few pages.

First of all, you have to realize that you don't need thousands, or hundreds, or even tens of JV partners. You've undoubtedly heard of the 80/20 rule, which says that 80% of your results come from 20% of your effort. Well, when it comes to affiliates and JV partners, it's generally more like the 99/1 rule, where 99% of your results come from 1% of your partners. In my business, we're extremely selective about who we take on as partners—we take on only top tier partners. And even so, the vast majority of our sales in any given launch will be generated by our top ten partners. It gets even more selective at the top, where the top three affiliates might generate a quarter of our sales. The way these numbers split out in any given launch will vary widely, but my point is that your top affiliates will generate the majority of your sales. And that means you don't need a lot of affiliate partners; you need only a few good ones. I often have students ask me how they can get a hundred or a thousand affiliates. I always tell them to not worry about getting a lot of affiliates but to get three to five high-quality partners that will really support them.

Finding potential partners is easy. They are the other people who are publishing in your market. Just type the top keyword search for your market into Google. For example, if your site is about teaching people to play guitar, just do a search for "learn guitar." Go to each of the top 50 listings and look around their site for a way to opt in. If they have an opt-in box, then they're building an email list, and they are a potential JV partner. At this point you should go ahead and join their list. Of course, if you join 50 lists (and you should), you're going to be getting a lot of email. You might want to set up a special email address for this so that your regular inbox won't be flooded with all that email.

After you're on those lists, watch what they send to their subscribers. Track who and what they're promoting. Watch to see if they promote only their products or if they promote products from other businesses. Evaluate the quality of their marketing as well as the quality of the relationship they're building with their list. Follow them in social media. Try to reverse-engineer their marketing and their offers.

What you're trying to do is create a target list of potential partners. Remember, you need only three to five high-quality partners, although you might need to approach 50 potential partners to find those few who are really going to rock for you.

As you go through this process, remember that good JV partners always have more people who are trying to get them to promote than they could possibly support. That's a reality of business. Their JV support is truly a scarce resource. So when you ask them to promote, you're just another hungry mouth looking for a meal. That means you need to create some value for them if you want to stand out.

One of the best ways to build value for potential partners is to have a great Launch Sequence that generates a lot of commissions for them. But even before you get there, you need to find other ways to create value just to get on their radar. One of the very best ways to build value for them is to promote their product first—if you generate a bunch of sales for them, then they will definitely take notice. Another easy thing you can do is buy their product, put it to use, and then give some constructive feedback and/or a positive testimonial. You can also give them regular feedback on their blog and in social media. The bottom line is that there are a hundred ways to create value for a potential partner—and the more value you create, the more you'll get back.

A Million Dollars in 53 Minutes

There are few things that can make as big an impact on your business (and your financial life) in as short a period of time as a successful JV Launch. And the impact goes far beyond the sales you generate in the launch. The long-term effect of the increased positioning in the market and the rapid list growth will reverberate in your business for years to come.

But if you're going to have success with JV Launches and JV relationships, then you absolutely must remember the two things I've hammered on throughout this chapter. First, you need to build long-term relationships with your JV partners. And second, you need to create real, long-term value for those partners. That doesn't mean it's going to take you years to build those relationships or that you are years away from doing a JV Launch. This can all happen surprisingly quickly, but it takes effort, and you should be thinking long-term.

When I did my first JV Launch, it literally created a business for me. That was the launch I mentioned at the start of this chapter, when I first rolled out Product Launch Formula in 2005 and the launch generated just over $600,000. I was instantly in business with sales, and I had a bunch of happy partners to whom I paid some big commissions. It also generated a list of more than 15,000 people. And it gave me huge positioning in the market. After that launch I was seen as one of the leaders in the industry, and Product Launch Formula was a recognized brand in the market. Sales continued to come in, and in my first year I did over a million dollars of sales. Those results all traced back to that initial JV Launch.

However, that was just setting the scene for what was to come next. In early 2008 I started working on an all new version: Product Launch Formula 2.0. I remade the product from the ground up based on everything I had learned since I first released PLF. In fact, it was going to be an entirely new offer, with greatly expanded content, over-the-top bonuses, and live coaching calls with me and my coaches. With this new offer, I increased the price to $1,997, and naturally it was time for another big JV Launch.

After two-plus years of supporting and nurturing my JV relationships, I had a lot of support to call on. During prelaunch, we generated over 34,000 opt-ins—a truly amazing number to get over a matter of days. As I reviewed all the data coming in during the prelaunch, it sure looked like it was going to be a great launch. But you just never know exactly what's going to happen, and as usual I had plenty of nerves going into launch day. It seemed like every possible JV in the known world was promoting my launch, and PLF had been a proven seller for years. But this was a new offer and a new price point, so I was plenty anxious.

Launch day was March 27, 2008. As usual, the days leading into launch day had been a blur. There's always a lot to be done, especially during a JV Launch. And the morning of launch day found me with my usual set of launch nerves, but I didn't have much chance to dwell on them; there were too many last-minute details to tend to. I remember that the minutes leading into the launch were complete chaos as we touched up the sales letter and the order form. And then it was time. All systems were go, and I hit the "send" button on the email.

I didn't have long to wait. The orders started coming in within seconds. They would pile in as fast as I could refresh the stats on my page. Later on, when I went back and analyzed the data, I found one single second where we had more than $12,000 in sales. $12K in one second! We hit a million dollars in sales in 53 minutes. And the sales didn't stop there. By the time I closed down the launch, after being open for only 34 hours, we were at $3.73 million in sales.

Of course, that wasn't all profit. By that time I had a small team of three contractors (although I was still working out of my home office and my team was all "virtual"). And I had affiliate commissions to pay. And there were other costs. Since I've always offered a generous money-back guarantee, I knew we would have some returns. But the numbers were still completely staggering. I clearly remembered how, just a few short years earlier, my ultimate dream for my business was to make an extra $10,000 a year to help support my family. Or even more recently, when I had to start over again after my first business imploded following that fateful call from my business partner. And now here I was sitting with a launch that did nearly $4 million in just 34 hours. Unreal.

That's the power of the JV Launch. It's just about the most powerful weapon in the whole PLF arsenal. There's only one thing that surpasses the JV Launch, and that's the Business Launch Formula . . .

Creating a Business from the Ether: The Business Launch Formula

Chapter 11

H ow do you reinvent a business when world events throw you a great big curveball? When someone flies a plane into a building and it jeopardizes your entire business model?

Ruth Buczynski is a licensed psychologist who runs the National Institute for the Clinical Application of Behavioral Medicine (NICABM.com). NICABM is a pioneer and leader in the field of mind-body-spirit medicine, and they've been an accredited provider of continuing education for health and mental health care professionals for over 20 years.

Since starting the company, Ruth has helped tens of thousands of psychologists, counselors, social workers, doctors, and nurses build their skills and better help their patients, primarily through live conferences. Her conferences had up to 1,000 attendees from around the world, and she brought in top experts to provide cutting-edge training.

Ruth's business was doing great until September 11, 2001. The terror attacks that day turned a lot of people's lives upside down, bringing about all kinds of unforeseen consequences. One of the impacts was that a lot of people started cutting back on their business travel. That hurt many businesses, including Ruth's. Her primary source of sales and revenue was her conferences—and it was becoming more and more difficult to convince people to get on a plane and travel to live events. While her business was still profitable, Ruth didn't like the direction in which her sales and profits were trending.

And life had another huge challenge in store for Ruth. Around that same time she lost her long-term partner to a lengthy battle with a terminal illness.

As Ruth emerged from a period of intense grieving, she looked at her business with fresh eyes, and she knew something had to change. Profits were down, and it was getting harder to fill her events. That's when Ruth looked to the Internet as a possible new path for her business. She decided to start creating "virtual" events instead of live, in-person events.

Ruth primarily sells to licensed practitioners. A small percentage of her clients are lay people, but most are accredited health care professionals. She offers continuing education credits for psychologists, physicians, nurses, counselors, and social workers. Her marketing needed to have a very professional look and feel but still make the sale. It was a perfect fit for the Product Launch Formula.

Surgeon General's Warning:
You Don't Know Who Is Watching Your Prelaunch

Ruth's online conference was successful right from the start. In many ways she runs a classic PLF launch for each of her summits. She'll publish three pieces of Prelaunch Content—generally videos, but occasionally a PDF report. For instance, in her recent "Brain Science" training, her first piece of PLC was a video, *The Two Things You Can Do Today for Your Brain*. That video generated more than 1,000 comments.

After Ruth runs a standard PLF-style prelaunch, she opens registration for her virtual event. The event is a series of webinars, and people can sign up and attend the webinars for free. Where Ruth makes her sales is at the "Gold" level, which includes the recordings of the webinars as well as transcripts and other bonuses.

It's worth noting that while Ruth is a licensed psychologist, she is not the "expert" in her trainings. Instead, she brings in world-class experts such as Daniel Amen, Ram Daas, and Daniel Goleman.

It's also worth noticing that Ruth actually gives away the bulk of her content—if you're willing to be on each webinar live, then you can listen to all of them without spending a single dollar. But lots of people pay for the extra benefits and bonuses that come with the Gold level.

Because of the success of this model, Ruth has expanded. She now holds three or four different virtual events a year, including one on mindfulness, a second on brain science, and another on the treatment of trauma.

To put this all in perspective—Ruth generates enormous numbers. In one of her recent trainings, she had 9,000 people (from 70 countries) logged in to listen to one of her webinars. Those numbers take on an even larger significance when you consider that the vast majority of listeners are licensed practitioners. Ruth is not really marketing to the general public, so she has a much smaller universe of people to sell to.

And Ruth recently saw another measure of her impact when she was invited to a meeting (along with other leaders in her field) to discuss ways to help the U.S. Army with mental health services for their troops. While Ruth was there she met the Surgeon General of the United States Army (a three-star general), who told Ruth, "I read your emails."

In other words, the Surgeon General of the U.S. Army was watching Ruth's Prelaunch Content!

Of course, the biggest news is that Ruth's business not only survived her transition from live, in-person seminars to webinar-based training, but it thrived.

Ruth Buczynski

In the last three years her business has grown by 160%, and she directly helps tens of thousands of people every year. And those health care professionals use Ruth's training to help hundreds of thousands of their patients.

Ruth's story is one of a complete reinvention of her business. The delivery of her product changed from a live conference to a virtual conference. Her marketing shifted from direct mail to an online-based launch. Along the way, she increased her profitability, expanded her reach, and lowered the risk in her business.

The Proven Formula . . . Expanded

Okay, so by now we've established that PLF is an incredible tool for launching your products and services. Now I want to talk about how to take it to the next level with what I call the Business Launch Formula (BLF). This is how you take the core Product Launch Formula concepts and use them to build (or grow) an entire business.

I've shared most of my personal story in the previous chapters—the crazy journey from Mr. Mom staying home taking care of a couple of babies to building a multimillion dollar business that's impacted hundreds of thousands of people. If I had sat down and written a novel telling this story, no one would believe it.

But the story is far bigger than me, because PLF is not just about launching products. It's about launching businesses . . . and even helping people create the life of their dreams.

You've learned about John Gallagher, whose family was on food stamps when he borrowed the money to get Product Launch Formula. He's now built a serious business that sells a whole line of products and employs six people.

And Susan Garrett, who has gone from being able to help just a few dozen people a year with their dogs to providing the same services to thousands of dog owners. Susan has also been able to drastically cut down on the amount of travel she needs to do, while increasing her income dramatically. In other words, she helps more people, has a better lifestyle, and makes more money—not a bad combination.

And Will Hamilton, who went from a just-out-of-college tennis instructor with a struggling tennis instruction web site to working with some of the top tennis pros in the world—helping them bring their knowledge and wisdom to the world.

Out of respect for my clients' privacy, I'm not going to disclose the types of financial results each of them are seeing in their business. But most people would find the size of their sales and profits downright shocking.

So how have they done it?

The Business Launch Formula

With my Product Launch Formula Coaching Program, I'm in the business of teaching people how to start and grow their businesses, specifically their online businesses. I teach them how to do that in the context of a product launch. But the reality is that the training goes much deeper. In fact, the way I like to think about it is that I help them reprogram their business DNA. Once they learn the strategies and tactics behind PLF, they usually start to apply those tools in every area of their business.

When someone comes into my PLF program, my personal goal for them is to do a year's worth of sales in a single week with their launches. That's a pretty lofty goal, and not everyone hits that goal. In fact, it almost never happens with their first launch. But the thing is, your first successful launch is not going to be your last launch.

And that's why there's an entire group of PLF students—like John Gallagher, Susan Garrett, Will Hamilton, and Ruth Buczynski—who take the launch to an entirely different level. They've used what I call the Business Launch Formula. This is the way it works . . .

Food Stamps to Six Figures (and Beyond)

Let's start with John Gallagher. As I told you earlier, his first launch was for a board game that taught kids about edible and medicinal plants and herbs. That launch generated a huge amount of goodwill, and it also helped add a lot of new leads onto his list. He took the momentum from that launch and used it to sell his herbal kit, which was a physical product containing the necessary components to create home remedies from herbs.

All of this helped raise his stature and positioning in the market, which in turn helped him build his list even more. And with each launch, the tremendous interaction with his list (i.e., the launch conversation) helped him pinpoint what his next product should be. Why guess about your next product when your prospects and clients are telling you what they want?

So at that point John put together a major new product: the membership site LearningHerbs.com. Naturally he did a launch for the site, and it was a huge success. He used all the knowledge and skills he had picked up from his earlier launches and had his best launch to date. He acquired hundreds of paying members for his site. Subsequent launches have raised that number of subscribers into the thousands. They each pay about $12 a month for access to the membership site.

That site gave him a very significant and automatic monthly recurring income—a revenue stream that he could count on. That regular revenue meant he could begin to hire people, and he slowly started to build his team.

That launch not only grew his list but expanded his positioning in the market. John is now a major player in the herbal education market. Of course, John has never positioned himself as the expert; he's more the person who brings the experts to his followers. Nevertheless on the business side of things, John is clearly a leader in his market.

That has allowed him to create video courses with some of the top experts in his niche. So now, a couple of times per year, John will launch an entirely new product that he co-creates with a top expert in the industry. In addition John will typically relaunch his membership site once per year. This means that two or three or maybe four times per year, John does a launch. And since he always delivers huge value in his prelaunches, each launch grows his list and his positioning in the market to an even greater degree.

When you're constantly delivering value into the market, you're constantly building a relationship with your clients and prospects. You're also stimulating the conversation with your clients and prospects, and that means you're always getting ideas for new products and promotions. And that's a winning formula for a continually expanding business. That's the Business Launch Formula.

A Dog's Life . . . Made Happier

Susan Garrett's version looks a little bit different, but the underlying strategy is very similar. When she first got her hands on the Product Launch Formula, her initial goal was to make enough money to pay for her PLF tuition before the credit card bill arrived. So she took a bunch of documents that she'd already written over the years and put them into a simple ebook she sold for $14.97. That initial launch made $27,000 in sales—considerably more than her tuition cost.

But the more important thing Susan took from her first launch was that the process worked. And with her competitive background, she knew she could get better at it—a lot better.

Shortly after her first launch, she produced a new training DVD. In the past her DVDs were primarily sold through distributors, but now that she had the beginnings of an email list, she decided to sell it herself. She put together a simple launch, and in three days she sold more DVDs than she had ever sold in an entire year through her distributor.

After that Susan decided to get serious about creating new information products. She's now created a series of video training products that are all offered online. With these digital products, she doesn't have to worry about the expense of producing DVDs or the hassles of working with a distributor. She sells her training courses direct to her clients, and they access them online.

She opens her trainings several times per year. She always uses PLF to deliver great value during her prelaunch—and to fill up her programs. And her business has grown to an impressive 16 times larger than it was before PLF. This has allowed her to build a small team that helps her continually increase the value of her trainings.

Along with the financial success of her business, Susan also has a simpler, nearly travel-free lifestyle. Now she travels only for competitions, so she's able to spend more time at home with her husband. Her success has allowed her to exponentially build her positive impact on the world and taken her closer to her ultimate goal of helping all dogs and dog owners lead happier lives.

From College Grad to New Media Mogul?

Will Hamilton's path in his business is yet another example of the Business Launch Formula. He started with a $35,000 launch—a huge win that gave him a viable business after a year of struggle. And he used what he learned in that launch to set up his next three launches that brought in a total of more than $340,000.

Those launches locked in his positioning as the leader in his market of online tennis instruction, and they dramatically built his list. No longer was he just some kid fresh out of college with a tennis web site. He had become a dominant player in the tennis instruction market.

Will's launch results and his positioning from those launches helped him land deals with top professional tennis players—first the Bryan Brothers (the all-time top pro men's doubles team), and then with Pat Rafter (formerly ranked #1 in the world). And that's not the end of the partnerships and deals; Will is in talks with other top pro players and is even considering moving outside of the tennis niche to work with pro athletes in other sports.

Launching: Not Just for Products Anymore

All four examples in this chapter show just how powerful the Business Launch Formula is—it's about building an entire business based on what you've learned in the Product Launch Formula.

The essence of PLF is giving first and asking for the sale later. You build a relationship as a trusted advisor (or even friend) before the transaction. You deliver great value, and you do it in a way that makes the sale before you've even asked for the order. In many ways, this isn't much different than what the very best sales people have always done for thousands of years.

However, with Product Launch Formula you're able to do that on a scale that really wasn't possible before. It's like combining the effectiveness of a face-to-face sale with the reach of television.

And no, it's not as effective as a great in-person sales presentation. And it doesn't have the reach of a huge TV network. But it brings much of the power and advantage of both.

And the Business Launch Formula is a natural extension of PLF. It's a matter of taking those principles of the launch and extending them to build an entire business.

Six Keys to the Business Launch Formula

Key #1: Always Deliver High-Value Prelaunch Content in Your Launches

First, you want to deliver high value into the market with your launches. That means delivering great Prelaunch Content that provides value all by itself, whether your prospect buys or not. This isn't news—I've hammered this point pretty hard throughout the book.

Not all your prospects will buy from you during your launch. In fact, in almost every launch the vast majority won't buy. There are lots of reasons why, but a common one is that the timing just isn't right. If you're selling wedding dresses, and your prospect isn't getting married in the next year, you're probably not going to make the sale.

However, in our current market where everyone can be a publisher in social media, where everyone can have an outsized voice if they so choose, the benefits of creating hundreds or thousands of raving fans is far reaching. The relationship you build during your launch can have an amplified effect. Each one of your prospects has a potentially viral impact on your business, so creating fans has never been more critical to your success.

And make no mistake—delivering real value in your prelaunch has a lasting effect. I've had people watch me through several launches before they were ready to buy. But when the time was right, they remembered me. I had delivered huge value and built up a significant level of trust, and they came back and bought.

Key #2: Always Be Building Your List and Building Your Relationship with That List

Once you have a warm list (even a small list of a few hundred subscribers), you realize that you are now in control of your destiny. The ability to write an email, send it to your list, and see the response within seconds will change what you think is possible. And at that point, you get very focused on building your list.

Of course, to even use the phrase "your list" is simplistic. As I mentioned in Chapter 3, you will have many lists. But in broad conceptual terms, I'm talking about your list universe, which will become the most valuable asset in your business. And to the extent that you build your list and your list relationship, you will build your business.

Every interaction with your list will either build on or detract from your relationship with the list. That doesn't mean that you should just send content and never ask for the sale. It means providing value AND making the sale. Remember that moving someone from being a prospect to being a client will increase the value of that relationship more than almost anything else. Once a prospect buys from you, they will be more likely to buy in the future, and they'll be more likely to buy at a higher price point. They will also be more likely to refer clients to you.

Key #3: Make More Than One Offer

It happens to almost everyone who goes through the PLF process. In the midst of your first launch, you get at least one great idea for your next offer or product. That's because of the launch conversation—your launch process creates a great deal of interaction with your prospects, and you'll get lots of ideas and suggestions. And many offers will likely lend themselves to periodic launches (such as Ruth Buczynski's annual summits). Often PLF Owners will do three or four launches per year and sometimes even more.

In my various businesses, I have found the sweet spot to be somewhere between two and four launches per year. Typically one or two of those launches have been big JV Launches (see Chapter 10) that dramatically build my list and make lots of sales. And the other launches are smaller Internal Launches that help me refine new offers and products before I roll them out as JV Launches.

Key #4: The Circle of Awesome: Seed to Internal to JV

There is a cycle of launches that works really well. I call it the Circle of Awesome. I know that's not the most grammatically correct term, but I invented it when I was with my son. And what it lacks in grammar, it more than makes up in, well . . . awesomeness.

It goes like this. You have an idea for a new product, so you use a Seed Launch to help birth the product. The Seed Launch (see Chapter 9) is great for getting your first few clients, making sure there's a demand, and creating a great product.

After the Seed Launch, you take the finished product and do an Internal Launch to your list. During your Internal Launch, you build out a full Prelaunch Sequence and really dial in your launch. By its very nature, the Internal Launch will usually bring you much greater financial results than your Seed Launch.

Then if you have good results with your Internal Launch, you move onto the JV Launch. You have the data and metrics from your Internal Launch to show to potential partners, and you have your Prelaunch and Launch Sequences largely done and tested. The JV Launch has a lot more moving parts, but since you've done most of the work already in your Internal Launch, it's a lot more manageable. And the results of a successful JV Launch are often exponentially larger than your Internal Launch.

And just to bring it full circle, after you go through that sequence of launches, you'll usually have several ideas for your next product. That's when you go back and test one of your new ideas with a Seed Launch and start the entire process over again. The only difference is that this time around you'll have significantly more experience, probably a much larger list, and lots of happy JV partners who will be ready to promote your next JV Launch.

It's one big circle, and it can be pretty awesome.

Key #5: Relaunches and Evergreen Launches

Relaunches can be very effective—just look at the way Barry Friedman did it (in Chapter 4). He ran his Showbiz Blueprint class over and over. The small class size kept the interaction level high, which meant he could charge a premium price. It also kept the demand high, so he was able to continue relaunching the offer.

Part of the effectiveness of your relaunches will be dependent on your ongoing list building. If you have new leads coming into your list, and you've got a proven Launch Sequence, then you've got a great opportunity. You can either run periodic relaunches, or you can use an Evergreen Launch.

Evergreen is really beyond the scope of this book, but it means that as new leads come onto your list, they will get to move through their own Launch Sequence based on when they joined the list.

Key #6: Take Care of Your Clients and Launch to Them Again

This is a universal truth of business: It's a lot easier to sell to someone who has bought from you in the past than it is to generate a new client.

The exact numbers on this vary, but they are always dramatic. Based on my experience in my various online businesses, it's about FIFTEEN times easier to sell to someone a second time than it is to get a new client.

That means you want to make sure you take care of your clients. I'm a big fan of over-delivering on my promises. This is something I plan out in advance. When I'm designing a new offer, I will actually hold back on some bonus items. I won't put them in the offer, nor will I talk about them during the sale. And then sometime after the purchase, I will surprise my clients with the extra bonuses.

Even the most grizzled customer is delighted to get an extra bonus that wasn't promised. And it's often shockingly easy to surprise and delight your clients—you don't have to get crazy to surprise and delight them when you're sending extra goodies.

It's not hard to impress your clients. Give them what you promised, give them great customer support, and then give them an extra surprise or two along the way. Do those things and you will be paid back 100 times. And your clients will not only be ready for your next launch, they'll be raving fans who support you during that launch.

The Formula That Launched a Thousand Businesses

The Business Launch Formula is a lot bigger than I could do justice to in this chapter. Out of necessity, this chapter is an overview from the 30,000-foot level. But this is the proven process I've seen my clients use over and over with consistent success. What they're doing is taking the Product Launch Formula and stepping it up to a higher level. Instead of a single launch of a product, it's a series of launches that create their business. Each launch builds on the success from the prior launch. The list gets bigger, the offers get better, there are more past buyers to sell to, the JV partner support gets stronger. That's the Business Launch Formula in action.

Creating a Business You Love

Chapter 12

A natural part of my business is that I get an inside peek into the workings of many businesses, and the entrepreneurs who create and run them. And that's what the next two chapters are about. It's one thing to build a business—but quite another to build a business and a life that you truly love. And I've noticed that a lot of people end up with a business they just tolerate. Worse are the people who build businesses they really don't like, or even hate. Either way, it's not a great situation.

It's understandable. Lots of people are like I was when I started out . . . desperate to get the business going and get their head above water. Any profitable business looks great when you're struggling to pay the bills and put food on the table.

But for most people, once they start to get the money figured out, the business becomes about more than just profits. That's when most people might ask, "Is this all there is?"

The way I look at it, if you're going to pour your heart and soul into a business, then you might as well create a business you love. One of the best things about having your own business is that you get to largely make up your own rules for the business, within legal and ethical boundaries, of course. So why not make up a set of rules that you can win by? Why not stack the odds in your favor?

And at the risk of my sounding like the carpenter who has only a hammer in his toolbox so everything looks like a nail, Product Launch Formula is the tool that will get you the business you love. But the first step is to figure out what you want your business to look like . . .

Your "Big Why"

To get to a business you love, the first thing you need to figure out is the "why" behind your business.

If it's just to get rich, that's fine. Making a lot of money is great. I like to think of money as stored up freedom and energy, and I love having lots of freedom and energy. As the saying goes, there are problems with having too little money and problems with having a lot of money. I like the problems that come from having money better.

What I've noticed about money is that once people get to a certain level of monetary success, they usually start looking for other things in their life. For example, a huge driver in my life is making a positive impact in the world, primarily through helping entrepreneurs. I know others who are driven to build a great team—to provide jobs and plenty of room for their employees to grow. Some people might be about creating great technologies. Or training people. Or reducing suffering.

I could go on, but you get the idea. At some point, there's usually a higher purpose than acquiring more money and stuff.

The thing is, it doesn't so much matter what your specific "why" actually is. The important thing is that you figure it out. As the saying goes, "If you don't know where you're going, any road will take you there."

In my PLF Live workshops, I have a process to get my clients to their "Big Why," and this is one of the most powerful exercises in the entire event. Once you get your "why" figured out, you become eminently more powerful.

Attract the Clients You Want

The reality is that not all people are created equal, and that's doubly true when it comes to clients. Some people will make great clients for you, and some won't. There will be people who resonate with your work, your products, your offers . . . and others who won't.

I'm not passing judgment on those people. I know some people will like me and my style, others won't. Some will think I'm not formal enough, that I'm too relaxed, that I should wear different clothing or be younger or older or whatever. That's okay, because I know that during my launch process I'll naturally attract clients who will end up being the kind of people that relate well to me.

In fact, I have this deep-rooted belief that I continually attract amazing people into my life.

Now I guarantee that some people will roll their eyes at that last sentence. Or they'll think that it's a silly conceit. But that's okay, because the odds are very strong that those are people who do NOT resonate with me. They won't be a good fit for me and my business. See how that works?

It will be the same for your business. All of us have people we connect with better than others. In fact, that's one of the jobs of good marketing—you want to attract the right people and repel the rest.

That word "repel" might turn off some people, but the last thing you want is a lot of prospects and clients who aren't a good fit for you. I've learned this lesson over and over. It was drilled into my head most recently when I spoke at two conferences. Both were large conferences with many hundreds of attendees. And on the surface, they seemed like they would have similar audiences who would be very receptive to my training.

The first group was wildly enthusiastic—and they hung on every word I said. They participated when I asked something of them. They were full of questions. The energy in the room was palpable. I loved every minute I was on stage, and when I finally stepped down I was swarmed by people asking questions for more than two hours.

I was on fire after that talk and looking forward to the second conference. Unfortunately, that turned out to be a very different room. The second group was attentive and respectful, but that was about it. I couldn't get them to participate. There were few questions. The room felt dead.

As I suffered through my presentation at that second conference, it couldn't have been more clear—the people in the first audience were "my people." Even though most of them had never heard of me before I walked on stage, they were a perfect fit for my message. On the other hand, the people in the second audience were clearly not my people. They were lovely people, but on the whole we just didn't fit each other.

The difference in those conferences was the marketing that put the people in the room. For the first conference, the marketing was very congruent with my approach to business. And, in retrospect, the opposite was true of that second conference. The marketing and messaging that put that second group in their seats was a pure hard sell—which is very different from the way I talk to my clients.

And the differences didn't stop in the conference room, because I tracked the people who became clients after those talks. The ones who came from the first conference were simply better clients. They required less customer support, they had a lower refund rate, they participated in the PLF community more, they got better results, they made better Case Studies, and they ended up joining my elite coaching groups at a higher rate.

The point of this story is this: You want to be sure you attract YOUR people into your business. Fortunately, you already have the tool you need to attract those people—the Product Launch Formula. When you follow the formula and authentically tell your story through your Prelaunch Content, you will attract your ideal clients. It's part of the process.

Look through the Corners

When my son first started racing mountain bikes, he learned an important lesson from his coach that he brought home and shared with me. He told me to "look through the corners." In other words, when you're on a bike hurtling down a steep mountain singletrack, you don't want to look at the trail directly in front of your wheel. That's a recipe for disaster. It means you'll always be reacting at the last second. Sooner or later you'll come to an obstacle where you won't be able to react quickly enough.

Instead, you need to extend your vision further down the trail. Move your horizon line as far out as you can. As you enter a corner, look through that corner to see where you're going to exit the turn. Even if the trees are blocking your view, focus intently and try to see through them for a clue to what's coming next. Look beyond the corner.

Business is the same way—you need to be looking further ahead than the next day or week or month. Don't chase every shiny object, don't be distracted by every new tactic. If you're going to change course or pursue a new direction, make sure you're doing so for a sound strategic reason.

I see too many people continually compromise their positioning, their brand, and their reputation by chasing after the latest tactic or the last dollar. It's downright sad to see people throwing away all the work they put into a business by focusing on the short term. The good news is that if you take the long view (and these days, the long view seems to be anything past the next three months), then you'll instantly stand apart in your market.

The Mastermind Principle

The idea of the "mastermind" is something Napoleon Hill wrote about in *Think and Grow Rich* all the way back in 1937, and it's an incredibly powerful concept. In fact, I wouldn't be where I'm at today if I hadn't actively engaged in several mastermind groups since the early days of my first business.

The way a mastermind works is simple: You get together with a group of like-minded entrepreneurs and you support each other in growing your business. This isn't a "networking group," although there is often some networking that naturally occurs as a byproduct of being in the group. It's all about sharing, brainstorming, and holding each other accountable.

Often there will be "hot seats," and if you haven't ever been through something like that, it's pretty wild. Basically, one person presents an idea or problem they have in their business, and then the entire group does a big brainstorm about the idea.

If you have the right people in the group, the hot seat usually ends up being like a massive shark feeding frenzy. When you put 20 or 30 creative entrepreneurs into a room and then throw a business problem in front of them, well, that's like putting blood in the water. And don't accidentally leave any arms dangling over the edge of the boat!

(And we all know it's much more fun to solve other people's problems than working on our own issues.)

I've been in a variety of formal mastermind groups over the years, starting in 1999. Some were paid memberships that are professionally facilitated. Others were groups of friends without a central facilitator. The formats varied—some were primarily email-based, others phone-based. And the most powerful revolved around in-person meetings.

I've also created high-end paid masterminds for small groups of my clients, which has given me deep insight into what it takes to create a great mastermind. (And my Platinum Mastermind has become a band of brothers and sisters to me. I've never experienced a more powerful, tighter community.)

What I've learned over the years (both from being a participant and an organizer) is that not all groups are created equal. There is no inherent magic in putting together a group of random people. It's all about the quality of the people and the level of community in the group.

A great mastermind has great people who are givers. These are people who focus on creating value for others before they look to take value. This is the very essence of a mastermind; everyone is there to focus on helping their fellow members, and they know their rewards will naturally come as part of the process.

However, being a giver isn't enough. You also need members who have the mental horsepower and the emotional intelligence to be able to contribute to the group at a high level. You don't want to be the smartest person in the room.

And the best masterminds have a strong ethos and an almost tangible sense of community. The group has a powerful sense of identity, and there's a feeling of "we're all in this together." I've been in groups where I feel a real sense of loss if I miss a meeting. If I'm offline for several days, the emails from the group will be the very first thing I look at when I get back to my computer.

When you get the right people and a great community, it's pure magic. As the saying goes, "A rising tide lifts all boats." And that's exactly what happens in a great mastermind. As each member focuses on helping the others in the group, they can't help but benefit. They end up getting the ideas, connection, and accountability that drives their business and life forward.

So here's my advice: Get in a strong mastermind. Ask other entrepreneurs you know for a recommendation of a group. There are some free (or nearly free) groups you can join, though they can be tough to find. They're almost always underground to some extent. The paid groups are usually easier to find (and they usually have a more formal structure). Or you can form a group yourself. You might have to try out a few groups before you find the one that's right for you. But the payoff is enormous when you find the right fit.

The Most Important Thing in Business

At a recent PLF Live workshop, I had an attendee come up and ask me what the single most important thing in business was, the one thing that has meant all the difference for me and my success, the one thing he should focus on as his business grows.

That's a really tough question! What's the one most important thing to focus on in your business? The one thing that makes all the difference?

My answer was this: opportunity cost.

Wikipedia says that opportunity cost is "the cost related to the next-best choice available to someone who has picked among several mutually exclusive choices."

That's a bit difficult to understand, in my opinion. I just think of it as "what you have to give up when you choose between two or more different choices."

And the cost is NOT restricted to financial cost. For an entrepreneur, the biggest opportunity cost is often time.

When you first start out, you will likely have limited capital. And since you'll be doing most everything yourself, you'll definitely have limited time. Picking the right opportunity is HUGELY important. Making the wrong choice can set you back weeks, months, or even years.

That's what opportunity cost is all about. You have to realize that chasing an opportunity has a greater cost than any financial expense it requires. I don't want to scare you into inaction, because taking no action has a HUGE opportunity cost. I just want you to realize that when you decide to go down one road, there are several other roads that you won't be able to go down.

And once you start to have success, then the issue of opportunity cost becomes even greater.

This is the deal. The more successful you become, the more "opportunities" you will have. This is what we call "deal flow." You start to have success, you build up a series of assets, you prove your worth—and all of a sudden everyone wants to do a deal with you.

And deal flow is a good thing. That's how the rich get richer. That's one of the reasons why it's easier to go from $100,000 to $1,000,000 than it is to go from zero to $1,000.

But as you get into the deal flow, it's easy to get distracted. You have only so much time, energy, attention, assets, etc., and every time you make a choice to pursue an opportunity, you are giving up something.

Usually, for entrepreneurs, that something is time.

I just heard my friend Dean Graziosi use this analogy to explain opportunity cost: It's like having a bookshelf that's completely full. If he finds another beautiful book he wants to buy . . . well, he can. But that means he has to get rid of one of the other books already on his shelf.

So remember . . . having choices in your business is great. But those choices have an opportunity cost. Making the right decisions around that opportunity cost is one of the biggest factors in the success of your business.

Don't Be Too Cool for School

If you're going to be in business, and you're going to have long-term success, then you need to be a perpetual student. Your market, clients, and competitors aren't going to stand still, and you can't afford to either.

In my business, I've gotten to know a lot of super-successful business owners, and I can tell you this: Everyone at the top is a constant learner. You can't be too cool for school.

Now that might sound self-serving since I'm in the business of teaching people about growing their business, but it's the truth. And the reality is that I spend a ton of time and money on my own education. I have to. It's my job. The payoffs in business are enormous, but one of the costs for great success is that you have to stay on top of your game.

You have to go to school. And you're going to have to keep going back to school.

No One Can Be an Island

This one is simple—you need to build strong relationships in your industry. In fact, even though I used the word "competitor" in that last section, I don't really use that word in my business. I think in terms of "partners" and "future partners."

I know there are some businesses where there truly is competition. For instance, if you own a gym, the odds are very strong that your clients are going to belong to only one gym. In that case, that would make the other gyms in your local area direct competitors.

But in the current market, with more and more people becoming knowledge workers, and more and more businesses becoming knowledge businesses, there are far more opportunities to cooperate than to compete.

My current business has literally been created by doing promotional partnerships with businesses that might be considered direct competition. But instead of competing, we support each other. The end result is that we don't have to worry about splitting up the pie. Instead we work together and grow a much bigger pie.

I suggest you start thinking of ways your competitors can become your partners. Try it out for a while, because your network is your net worth.

You Need to Be in the Information Business

In this book, almost all of the examples I've used have been "information businesses"—businesses that deliver a product that teaches or trains people about something. It could be dog training or tennis or juggling.

But not every business will be an information business. After all, someone needs to sell cars or real estate or clean people's carpets.

However, in our current world, nearly everyone needs to be in the information business to some degree. And adding an information component to a business—either as part of the selling process or as part of the product—will become a huge part of almost every successful business.

For instance, Joe Polish initially grew his carpet cleaning business by offering a free report that educated consumers on the fraudulent selling techniques that many carpet cleaning businesses used. That report ended up generating a huge amount of exposure and sales for his business. He didn't have an information business, but he used a knowledge product to build his offline service business.

We live in a connected, information-rich world. People expect to be connected and to have information at their fingertips. And in that environment, nearly every business should be in the publishing business at some level . . . either as part of their marketing or as part of their offer.

The Human Touch

This is something I stumbled onto when I started my first business back in 1996—it's a lot easier to sell with the human touch. I've always been happy just being me and not pretending to be some big corporation. I never referred to myself as "we" in my emails, and that set me apart from the very beginning. Back in the early days, everyone was trying to sound like some big important company, but I wrote my emails to the people on my list in the same voice I would use when writing to my friends. It worked.

People want to connect with people, not faceless corporations. They don't want to get an email written in what I call "the corporate voice" or "airline speak." You know what I'm talking about: "The aircraft door is now closing. Please read the safety card that has been placed in the seat pocket in front of you." This sounds cold, impersonal, officious. Sure, there are rare exceptions; if you're in a mission-critical situation, your clients will want to know that you have the resources to back up your services. But even then, they'll still want to interact with a human.

That "corporate voice" is death to sales. People want to buy from people. Forget the royal "we" when speaking to your clients. Talk to them one on one. This will make it easier to sell your stuff, and running your business will be a lot more enjoyable. Again, the PLF process is all about creating a connection and a conversation with your prospects, and communicating in a way that builds a relationship with your new clients.

Playing by Your Rules

Having a great business starts with realizing that you're in control. This might sound obvious, but so many people create a business that's modeled on other businesses they see. Or what they think a business is supposed to look like.

Remember, you get to make up the rules. You don't have to do business the way the other people in your market do business. You don't have to do business with clients you don't like. You can create a business you love.

And it all starts with getting clear on what that business looks like and what your life would look like if you had that business. That's what the next chapter is all about . . .

A Recipe for a Big Life

Chapter 13

fter I graduated from Michigan State University with a business degree, I landed a job with Motorola in Tempe, Arizona. I had a couple different job offers, but I picked Motorola mostly because I liked the location. I grew up in the Detroit area, and I had never been west of the Mississippi River, but I had always felt a pull to move out West.

It's a long drive from Michigan to Arizona. It took me four days. On the third night, I stayed in a tiny hotel in a town I'd never heard of—Durango, Colorado. I had never seen mountains like that in my life, and I was impressed. In the morning I called my parents to tell them about my trip so far, and I couldn't stop talking about Durango.

After a few minutes, my dad said, "Wow, it sounds like you just want to stay in Durango and not go any further." After all these years, I still remember him saying that, because it struck me as such a ludicrous idea at the time. The idea of my living in Durango seemed about as likely as me walking on the moon.

I grew up in a wonderful, supportive family. My parents did a great job raising my siblings and me. They gave us a good start in life and made sure we went to college. And the pattern for my life seemed to be set: get an education, find a "good job," and then work at that job for the rest of your life. That's what all my extended family did. That's what all my friends' families did. That's what everyone in my middle-class suburban neighborhood did.

For some reason, though, I'd always had a yearning to own a business. I have no idea where that came from, but I remember having that strong desire even when I was 10 years old. But I had no role models for starting and building a business. I had no frame of reference. I didn't know how people actually did something like that. It went against everything I saw in my life. So off I went to Tempe to follow that familiar pattern for the rest of my life.

But once I got to Tempe and I started my job at Motorola, I quickly learned I didn't fit in the corporate world. I was a round peg trying to fit into a square hole. It just didn't work. And that's a big reason why, just a few years later, I found myself quitting my job, walking away from the corporate world, and staying at home to take care of a couple of young children. I had washed out of the corporate world, never to go back.

Moving to Durango

I'm typing this to you from my hometown of Durango, Colorado. My wife and I moved our family here 14 years ago. My dad was right all those years ago when he said it sounded like I wanted to live in Durango. I live here because I can live anywhere in the world that I want.

My business is 100% online, and my team is virtual, so that effectively uncouples my business from the constraints of geography. I can work anywhere I have an Internet connection.

Durango might not be most people's first choice, but I love it. The most beautiful mountains in Colorado are almost in my backyard, and the great deserts of the American Southwest are just a couple hours away. I have easy access to great skiing, incredible mountain biking, and beautiful river trips. I love the people who choose to live in Durango, and it's been a fantastic place to raise our kids.

Each morning, I get up when I wake up. The only time I set an alarm is when I want to get up to the mountain early on a ski day. Or if I need to catch an early flight. (I travel only when I want to—if it's for business, I'm on my way to meet some amazing people or go to a world-class training.)

Part of the joy of living in Colorado is sharing my passion for the outdoors with my kids. Both of them are great mountain bikers and skiers, and they've been down some of the greatest wilderness rivers in the world.

I don't tell you any of this to brag—I just want you to understand what's truly possible in your life. I've got a business that's helped thousands of entrepreneurs, I've got a great team that enables me to run the business, we've got raving fans for clients, I have an income beyond anything I could have dreamed of, I get to live where I want . . . and I still have the time to enjoy the beautiful outdoors just outside my door.

Of course, sometimes when people hear this, they think it's just that I'm truly special. Or maybe I've got some magical powers. Or I had some insider connections. Or I got inordinately lucky.

Unfortunately, I have no magic powers. And when I started this business I had no connections whatsoever. And I certainly didn't start with any advantage or any money.

So how did I go from a simple Midwestern boy, corporate failure, Mr. Mom, to having the life of my dreams?

It's because of the business I created with the Product Launch Formula. Sure, there's been plenty of hard work and more than a few lucky breaks, but it's all in the formula.

And here's the thing—I'm not the only one who's done it. Many of my students and clients have achieved similar results. You've already read about several of them in this book.

So how do you build a business and a life where you can live where you want, work when you want, have the lifestyle that you want?

Start with the Vision

When I was about to start my first business, I went through an exercise where I created my ideal life in my mind. I read about this exercise in a training product, and I think this is what set up all my success. It didn't take long and was easy to do. I wrote down everything I wanted—income, lifestyle, material things, travel experiences. The list wasn't very long because I had no idea of the possibilities back then. Compared to my lifestyle now, my vision was very modest, but that list gave me the direction I needed.

The funny thing is, as soon as I finished the exercise, I tucked the list away in the back pocket of my journal and forgot about it. Then a couple of years later I stumbled across the list—and realized I had achieved nearly every single goal I'd written down. That's when I became a real believer in creating that future vision of my life in my mind . . . and writing it down.

Once my business started growing, I rapidly revised and added to the list. I wrote down everything I wanted in my future: my target income, the amount of time I could be away from my business, how I'd spend my free time, the state of my finances, what I'd be doing in my business, the impact I'd make with my business, the type of people I'd work with, etc.

If you choose to go deeper, you can write down what you want in your future relationships, physical and emotional health, education, home, family, etc.

It's important to understand that there is no right or wrong answers when you go through this exercise. And what you write down is not forever; you can change it at any time—and you most definitely will. This is your ideal vision of your future life right now. You can do this exercise for any time frame you want, but I usually use three years or five years from the present. Remember, this list is a work in progress. I'm continually updating my vision for my future life, and you should do the same.

So go ahead and do it. Turn off your phone, your email, your instant messenger. In fact, it's probably a good idea to just turn off your Internet connection. Trust me, everything will still be there when you turn them back on in 30 minutes. Close the door, or get out of your home and go to a coffee shop or library. Use paper and pencil or open up a blank document on your computer. Write down what your ideal life will look like in three years:

What your income will be
What kind of car you will drive
Where you will live and in what kind of home

Who your clients will be and how you will serve them

What your physical and mental health will be like

What your relationships will be like—with your friends, partner, kids, parents, coworkers, etc.

What your spiritual life will be like

What trips and experiences you will have

What you will have accomplished personally and professionally

One more hint: This is more powerful if you write everything down as if you've already achieved it.

Don't underestimate this process. Everything significant you create will first be created in your mind's eye.

Now that you're clear on where you're going, let's talk about some specifics of how to get there . . .

The Security of Being an Entrepreneur

To create the life of your dreams, the first thing you need is security. Lots of people who are thinking of starting a business worry about leaving the security of the paycheck world.

Unfortunately, there is no longer any security in a paycheck. I'm sure you know of people who worked loyally for a company for many years, only to be laid off or have the business close its doors and shut down.

The world has changed, and the only true security is your ability to create value and get paid for that value. Once you create your own business, you understand what security truly is. Even after I lost my first business to a partnership breakup, it took me a matter of weeks until I was back on my feet and had started a new business.

The greatest investment you will ever make is the investment in your business skills. When you can create a new business from the ether, then you control your destiny. And of all the business skills you can have, the one skill that pays off better than any other is the ability to market and sell yourself and your business.

And it should come as no surprise that I think PLF is the best way to sell in this day and age.

Sharpen the Saw

This was one of Stephen Covey's seven habits for personal success—you need to take time away from work to recharge and refresh. You can't continually operate at a high level if you're working 100% of the time. No one can always be operating at peak efficiency and creativity. Unfortunately, I see lots of entrepreneurs creating a life where they do nothing but work. They literally never take a day off.

There's an old joke among entrepreneurs about the biggest benefit of owning your own business. The punch line is that you only have to work half-time—any twelve hours of the day that you want.

That's not healthy. In the long run, your business and your life will suffer for it. And it's not a recipe for living a big life.

Sure, there are always going to be some long days—especially when you're starting out. But if you never have time away from your business, then you're doing something wrong.

My friend Joe Polish uses the analogy of a race horse. If you owned a million-dollar racehorse, you would exercise great care in how you treated that horse. You would feed it well, make sure it was well-rested, carefully monitor its workouts, give it a clean, comfortable stable, and schedule regular checkups with a vet.

In your life and your business, your body is your million-dollar racehorse. Don't you deserve the same care?

I don't want to get into belief systems, but most of us would agree that we only get one shot at this life . . . at least in our current form. So how are you going to spend that one precious life? Are you going to take care of your multimillion dollar body and mind?

Will you make sure you eat healthy, nutritious food? Get enough sleep? Get outside? How about exercise? Meditation? Stretching or yoga? Regular health checkups?

Working more hours is not the answer to your problems. You need to work better and smarter, and one of the keys to doing that is continually refreshing your mind and body. You need to sharpen the saw.

We're in the Himalayas

One thing you can't avoid when you become an entrepreneur are the highs and lows in your business. Of course, that happens to everyone whether or not they have their own business, but for most people the highs will get higher and the lows will get lower when they become an entrepreneur.

Most of us wouldn't trade this life for anything—we love the control we have over our destiny. We love not answering to anyone. We love being able to create. We love the big wins. But we know that we won't win every time; there are going to be some lows.

My friend Lisa Sasevich likes to say we live in the Himalayas—as entrepreneurs, the peaks and valleys are bigger than they are for other people. When we strap on our entrepreneur super hero outfit, life is different for us than it is for normal civilians.

That means we have to be careful to manage our mental states. It's one thing to have a bad week or two if we've got a paycheck job—in most cases, the paycheck will keep coming in. But if we're running our own business, and especially if we have a team that's depending on us, we need to be able to pull ourselves out of the funk.

And, of course, I'm no different than anyone else. I have my share of ups and downs. But what I've done is create a process for this. I keep a list of things that will pull me up when I'm not in peak state. Everyone will have their own list, but after comparing my list with those of many of my students and colleagues, I've noticed there's often a lot of overlap.

Here's a partial list of the stuff that works for me. Take what works for you, leave the rest:

Exercise: This is at the top of the list. Nothing changes my state for the better more quickly than getting my heart rate up. It's even better if it's outside (as opposed to being in a gym).

Meditate: This is a close second to exercise. It doesn't have to be complicated, just close your eyes and focus on your breath. Five minutes is all you need, but twenty minutes is even better.

Get outside: Few things will lift me up faster than being outside in nature.

Have an adventure: Go on a big mountain bike ride, have a big ski day or surfing day. Go for a hike. Visit a museum. Travel.

Serve or give: Do something good for someone else. I think it's impossible to feel sorry for yourself when you're acting selflessly and helping other people.

Be grateful: Few things will lift you up faster than recognizing and feeling gratitude for all the many good things in your life, which are sometimes easy to overlook. Take time to sit down and list all your blessings. You might want to start with your breath and your life . . . they're not something to take for granted.

That's my list, or at least part of it. Yours will probably be different. I'm an introvert. If you're an extrovert your list will probably look quite different. What's important is that you recognize when you're in a funk, and you have a strategy for lifting yourself out of it.

Stay in Your Genius Zone

My coach Dan Sullivan (of Strategic Coach®) talks about the concept of Unique Ability®. What's the one thing (or two or three) you were put on earth to do? What can you do so well that time seems to disappear when you're doing it?

What do you do that other people find exceptional but comes so easily you can't understand why they're so amazed?

Those are the things in your genius zone, or your Unique Ability®.

In your business, you want to work on those things at which you're great. Don't spend your time on the stuff that's difficult for you. Work on your strengths, not your weaknesses. Hire people to do the things that are not in your genius zone.

Once you get rid of activities you aren't good at, the next thing to eliminate are the things you are proficient at but still aren't in your genius zone. Again, other people are better than you at those jobs, so hire them. Eventually, you will eliminate the tasks you are excellent at—because even though you're excellent at them, they still aren't in your genius zone. Doing those things takes you away from doing your genius activities.

The more time you spend in your genius zone, the better for you, your business, your clients . . . and the world.

Your Most Scarce Resource

Your most scarce resource is focus.

The world will conspire to distract you. Your phone, email, text messages, instant messenger, social media, and more will all pull you away from what you should be doing.

Many people wake up and instantly look at their phone. They check messages, check email, check various social media. That's a huge mistake—the only thing that's waiting in your phone is someone else's agenda. If you check your phone or your email right away in the morning, you've lost control of *your* agenda. There will be emails or messages waiting for you to respond, and once you start responding you've lost control of your day.

You should start the day by focusing on your highest-value activities before you get caught up in other people's agendas for you. What are your highest-value activities? The ones that are in your genius zone or a Unique Ability®.

Clients You Love

I mentioned this in the last chapter, so I'm not going to spend a lot of time on it, but having great clients whom you love working with and serving is a fantastic shortcut to loving your life.

I frequently hear people complain about their clients—but the thing is, they're the person who picked those clients.

Remember, if you want different clients, then change your business, change your product, change your messaging, change your marketing. You're the one attracting those clients, and making the decision to work with them . . . so pick great ones.

My highest-level clients are the people in my Platinum Mastermind group, and I love spending time with them. It's a small group that I meet with several times a year, and space in the group is severely limited. To get into Platinum, members go through a rigorous application process. My team and I screen for people who fit the group culture and who I really want to spend time with. Every time I leave one of those meetings I'm more energized than I was at the beginning of the meeting. In fact, I try to set up my schedule so I always have a Platinum meeting directly before I lead one of my large workshops, because I know the meeting will leave me on fire with energy as I head into the big workshop. As I type this, we're in our fourth year with Platinum, and many of the members have been with me since the beginning.

Of course, that's just one example—the larger point is this: You control who your clients are. You do that through your market selection, offer selection, and marketing.

Don't compromise on this. Attracting new and better clients is what Product Launch Formula is all about. Now go get the clients you want.

You Can't Get There Alone

When I started out, I had this fantasy that I could build my business all by myself.

I figured my life would be a lot simpler that way, and since it was a virtual business with a virtual product, I figured I could really scale up the business without creating a team.

In fact, I didn't hire anyone or use any contractors for the first 10 years I was in business. That was a big mistake, and it ended up holding me back. I now see that was about as mature as a two-year-old saying, "I can do it all by myself!"

The reality is that you can't build anything great by yourself. And if you even try, then you're going to be spending huge chunks of time working outside your genius zone.

Once you start building a team, your life will get more complicated. That's inevitable—any time humans are involved, things get more complicated. You will have to learn to be a leader for your team (if you don't already have that skill). And in many ways, you will have to answer to your team.

One thing that will make this process a lot easier is if you stick to a policy that my friend Eben Pagan calls "stars only." In other words, you want to hire only stars—the people who are in the top 10% of any skill set. In fact, you should probably take this further and hire only those people who are in the top 1% of any skill set.

Stars will make your life easier. They will be self-motivated. They will require less supervision and training. They will have less drama in their life. If they're good at their skill set, but they've got a lot of drama, then they're not stars.

The Magic Word

As you become more successful, there's one word that will become more important than any other. That word is "no."

As Warren Buffett said, "The difference between successful people and very successful people is that very successful people say 'no' to almost everything."

In Chapter 12 I said that the idea of "opportunity cost" is the most important consideration in business. That's what we're really talking about here, but on a more personal level. As you become more successful, build more personal power, and grow into the role of leader, other people will find you more attractive. It can't help but happen—it's automatic. There's a huge vacuum of leadership in the world right now, and people are looking for leaders to plug into and follow.

The next step is that more people and more deals start to pop up in your life. Many of the opportunities will be very attractive and would have impressed you if you'd had those same opportunities earlier in your life.

However, you must be very careful about what you say "yes" to. You have to become increasingly more selective. You need to get better at saying no. Anything that doesn't advance you toward your future and your bigger vision for yourself is something that will take you off your path.

I'm not saying you can't be a friend. I'm not saying you have to abandon the people and things that got you where you are. And I'm certainly not saying you can't lend a helping hand. You just have to be very careful of your time and your energy. Every new opportunity you say "yes" to closes the door on another opportunity.

Drinking the Abundance Juice

When I first started publishing my free investing newsletter in 1996, there was another web site publishing a very similar newsletter. However, even though we targeted the same niche, our sites were very different. They charged for their newsletter; mine was free. They had a much more professional-looking site; mine was very amateurish. In fact, back then I couldn't even afford to buy a domain name or web site hosting, so my site was hosted on a free server.

That competing site was published by a guy named Frank Collar. I would often look at his site and wander through all the pages. It was my ultimate dream to have a professional site like that and publish a paid newsletter like he did. But I didn't know how I would get there. I didn't know any of the tech stuff required and I didn't have money to hire the people who did. And I didn't know how to sell stuff. Most important, I didn't have the confidence to ask people to buy my stuff.

In any case, one day I got an email from Frank. He asked me how I put together some of the stock market charts on my web site. That email gave me a shock. I was surprised that Frank even knew who I was or that my site even existed, so on one level I was flattered.

On another level, Frank was a direct competitor. It was like he was Coke and I was Pepsi (although in reality, I was more like some generic cola). We were in the EXACT same business. And those charts on my site were the only thing that was pulling in traffic to my site. These days, it's a simple thing to post an image like a stock chart to a web site, but it was a different world back then. I'd spent the better part of a day and more cash than I could afford figuring out how to do it. I had invested time, effort, and hard-earned money to create those charts on my web site, and I saw them as my one major asset in my business.

So as I looked at that email from Frank, I wondered what to do. Should I give him my trade secret? Should I turn him down? Or should I just ignore his email?

In the end, I decided I might as well help him out. I knew that if I had figured it out, he would certainly be able to. And why put him through the day of tedious trial-and-error that I went through to learn how to do it?

So I took 20 minutes and I typed up a complete set of instructions for how I created and posted my charts, and I sent the email off to Frank.

Within just a few minutes I got an email back from Frank thanking me. He went on to tell me that he had many years of newsletter publishing experience in the offline world, and he had done a lot of testing of his online newsletter. He shared a lot of great information about some of those tests—including some critical pricing tests. And he went on to tell me that if I ever wanted to publish a paid newsletter, then he would be happy to help me out with his knowledge and experience.

In that moment, when I read that email, my life changed.

I realized that we were operating in a brave new world, where in many (most?) cases, cooperation was more important than competition. Years later, I would coin the term "Abundance Juice" to describe this phenomenon.

Simply put, you have the choice between an abundance-based mindset and a scarcity-based mindset. Choose wisely, because your choice will impact every area of your life. In my experience if you pick the abundance mindset, there's a lot more joy, fulfillment, and . . . well, abundance.

A few months later Frank did indeed help me launch my paid newsletter. His advice and experience gave me the confidence to create that newsletter, and it became a huge success for me. (That was the $34,000 launch I told you about in Chapter 1.) Then a couple of years later, when he was tired of publishing his newsletter, Frank actually GAVE me his list of paying subscribers. I took over servicing his subscribers and made a lot of money doing so. All because I had helped him out with a simple favor. All because I had shared the Abundance Juice with him.

One of my core beliefs is that you will be far happier if you drink the Abundance Juice and adopt the abundance mindset. And in addition to being happier, your business will grow faster and larger, you will attract better clients and partners, and you'll have a much bigger positive impact on the world.

So I invite you . . . go ahead, drink the Abundance Juice.

A Life Well Lived

In my opinion, there is no other business building system with more amazing success stories in the last decade than Product Launch Formula. I have walked you through the entire formula in the pages of this book. In other words, I've given you the tool to create your business.

But, as the saying goes, with great power comes great responsibility. I've given you a lot of power.

But make no mistake—building a successful business will not automatically lead to a happy and fulfilled life. There's plenty of miserable entrepreneurs out there. The trick is to create a business AND have a great life. To get there, you need to be intentional with the business you build and the life you create. It doesn't happen by accident.

Dancing Your Way around the World

Sebastien Night was born in French-speaking Guadalupe in the Caribbean, and he now lives in France. He first went through my training in 2010. Since then he's been using PLF to build his business. Initially he was in the French "dating advice" market, where he taught shy men how to approach women and ask for a date. Eventually, Sebastien transitioned to teaching French-speaking people how to build their online businesses, and he's now known as "the French Marketer." Sebastien has done dozens of launches, and he's built up a serious business. In fact, he's one of the most prominent online publishers in the French-speaking world.

As with any entrepreneur, he's put in a lot of work to get to where he's at. But he's also created an incredible lifestyle. A high point so far is that he was able to fulfill two lifelong dreams of his fiancée, Cecile—dancing and traveling around the world.

Last year Sebastien took a six-month trip around the world with Cecile, and they danced the entire way. They visited Australia, Brazil, India, Argentina, South Africa, Thailand, Durango, and New York. While they were in India, Sebastien proposed to Cecile—and she said yes!

During the trip Sebastien worked one day per week. Like mine, his business is completely virtual, so he could work anywhere in the world. The entire trip was financed by one of his launches, and he's also going to be paying for two great weddings (same bride for both, but one in France and one in Guadalupe).

The thing is, if you pull Sebastien aside, he'll tell you that the most exciting part is that he has friends and family who have seen his success, and they're now following his example and creating their own businesses.

(To see my Case Study with Sebastien, as well as the video of his round-the-world trip with Cecile, go to http://thelaunchbook.com/sebastien.)

It's Your Time to Launch

Chapter 14

So that's the Product Launch Formula.

Now it's your turn. The formula has been proven thousands of times over. All of my personal success has been built by doing exactly what I taught you in this book. I've built several businesses now, and every one of them was based on the Product Launch Formula. In fact, I launched the latest one just a few weeks ago, and it got off to another roaring start, thanks to the very strategies I've laid out here.

What's more important is that this is the exact formula my clients have used to generate more than $500 million in sales. That's a half-billion dollars in success stories. They've done it in nearly every market or niche you can think of, with products that range from cage fighting to meditation workshops to tax preparation to marching band accessories.

Death of Launches

Back when I first published PLF in 2005, the online marketing community was still a relatively small one. Most of the big players knew each other. And it took only a few months until some people started talking about the "death of launches." That was the exact phrase used in a major white paper that came out less than a year after I released PLF. Some of those "in the know" predicted that the PLF model was so powerful, it would collapse under its own weight. Conventional wisdom said that once everyone in the marketplace had seen a launch or two, the whole launch idea would stop working. As the old quote goes, "We have met the enemy and he is us."

The truth is, the launches have only gotten bigger and better since then. A more apt quote would be "The reports of my death are greatly exaggerated."

So what happened?

Tactics Come and Go, Strategy Is Forever

Military (and business) leaders nearly worship *The Art of War* by Sun Tzu. The book is thousands of years old, but that doesn't stop every new generation of leaders from reading it. That's because the book is about strategy, not tactics. And strategy never goes out of style.

The reason PLF keeps working is that it's based in strategy. I teach plenty of tactics as part of the formula, but those tactics are always used to serve the overall PLF strategy. And frankly, tactics come and go. For example, when I first started doing launches, streaming video didn't exist. For that matter, blogs didn't exist. Nor did social media or webinars. But now we use all those tools in our launches.

Tools change, tactics change. Strategy endures.

Creating a close connection with your prospect will never go out of style. Building up the anticipation for an event will never go out of style. Mental triggers such as social proof, authority, community, and reciprocity will never go out of style. Building influence by delivering massive value before you ask for the sale will never go out of style. The exact way you actually deploy those things has changed and will continue to change. But the PLF strategy keeps working.

Turn Your Computer into a Money Machine

Sometime around 1994—I don't recall the exact date—I received an advertisement for a product called "Turn Your Computer Into a Money Machine." Now, I'll admit that's a pretty cheesy name, but it caught my attention enough so that I opened it up and started reading. I suppose I was in the perfect target market for the ad at the time—this was back when I was in my stay-at-home dad phase. We were struggling to make ends meet, and I really needed any kind of a money machine I could get.

The ad arrived via email, and it was really long—it must have been 10 pages or more. After I read it through once, I felt like I needed to read it again, so I printed it out on my dot matrix printer. Because that printer was slow and the ad was so long, it seemed to take forever to print.

Over the next week I read that ad over and over. It talked about creating "special reports" and selling them online. It talked about the wonders of having a publishing business and selling direct to consumers.

The idea seemed nearly unbelievable to me. However, the publishing business had been around for centuries, so I figured it had to be profitable. And I knew of small, independent publishers who seemed to be making money. For example, when I looked for books on some of my interests like whitewater kayaking and mountain biking, all the popular ones came from small publishers who were grassroots, mom-and-pop businesses.

On the other hand, I had never created or published anything in my life. And even more frightening was the very idea of selling. I had no experience in sales. In fact, if I listed the absolute most unlikely possible career choices for myself, sales would probably be at the top of the list.

And there was another big problem—"Turn Your Computer Into a Money Machine" cost $99.50. At that time we were supporting a family of four on Mary's lone paycheck from her government-funded job. When I put together a budget for our family, we had a little more than $400 left as disposable income per year. Spending nearly a quarter of our yearly "spending money" on something like this felt like a risky proposition.

But that ad made so much sense. The entire idea made so much sense. And I was desperate for a change. I spent a full week reading through that ad again and again. Every night I would lie in bed thinking about it. I would wonder if it could possibly work for me. What could I publish about? Would I actually follow through and do it? Would I be able to sell anything? Or would it be another failure in my life?

Perhaps you've been in a similar place before, wondering about a potential fork in the road. Lots of times, I procrastinate when it comes to making decisions.

But this was one time I acted. I suspended my disbelief, filled out the order form, and mailed it off.

The Road Less Traveled

Robert Frost has an elegant and very famous poem about paths taken and not taken. And it seems a bit silly and a little grandiose to invoke that poem when I'm telling you about answering a direct mail ad. But that one action made all the difference.

The product was simple—it came on a single 3.5-inch floppy drive. It taught the basics of direct marketing for information products. It was mostly about selling stuff on CompuServe and AOL—a couple of old, online services that acted as something of a gateway drug to the Internet back in the early 1990s.

It might have been old school, but that one information product opened up a whole new world for me—the world of direct marketing and creating an online, information-based business. And that world has been amazingly good to me. Of course, the money and success didn't come instantly, or even quickly for that matter. But it did come . . . and you wouldn't be reading this book if I hadn't answered that ad.

A number of years ago I sent an email to Sheila Danzig, the creator and publisher of "Turn Your Computer Into A Money Machine." I told her what her product had done for my life, and the impact it had made on my family. It was a joyful email for me to send, and I heard back from her the next day. She was thrilled to get my email and hear how she had contributed to my success.

I know that feeling, because I get those types of notes and emails from my PLF students and clients every week—and reading those success stories never gets old.

Just this morning I received an email from Franz Weisbauer, a Fulbright Scholar and a doctor in Vienna, Austria. He's an internist with a clinical specialization in echocardiography (ultrasound of the heart). In 2010, he created an online training platform (along with his colleague Dr. Thomas Binder) to teach echocardiography to doctors and sonographers. Normally, this type of training would require traveling to three weekend seminars that cost $500 each. The story of this launch is not unlike many you've already read in this book. When Franz and Thomas first released the program with "Hope Marketing," they had few sales. They had a great product, but it wasn't selling at a level to make it a viable, ongoing business. Then Franz heard me speak about product launches at an event. He enrolled in my PLF training at the next opportunity and relaunched his site with a full PLF-style launch. The launch was a huge success and completely transformed his business. And it didn't end with his initial launch—the business has grown to ten times its pre-PLF level. But volume of sales is only one measure of the success of a business. It's an easily calculable one, but numbers don't always paint the whole picture. Another measure is the impact—the number of lives that have been saved by the doctors and sonographers who have gone through Franz's training.

It's that ripple effect that gets me so excited that sometimes it's hard to sleep at night. I taught Franz how to launch his product, then his training helped thousands of doctors to treat tens of thousands of patients (and saved lots of lives along the way). Who knows the positive effect all those patients, with a new chapter added to their life, will have on the world?

Your First Launch

The next step is up to you. My goal in this book was to show you the process. A secondary goal was to make you realize that you can do this. I've seen it work over and over for my students . . . students from every walk of life and from all around the world.

The key is to take that first step and to keep taking baby steps. If I can go from Mr. Mom with zero entrepreneurial experience to tens of millions of dollars in sales, you can certainly do it as well. If John Gallagher can go from food stamps to a six-figure business, you can do it as well. If Tara and Dave Marino can go from heartbroken parents to a half-million dollars in sales, you can do it as well.

Don't expect to make a million dollars with your first launch. Don't expect to equal some of the outsized results I've told you about in this book. Don't compare yourself to my million-dollar launches. Compare yourself to my first launch that did a modest $1,650 in sales.

Expect to make some mistakes and learn a lot. Expect it to be a lot more work than you anticipate. Expect some frustrations and some late nights.

And expect your first launch to be unforgettable.

A Long Strange Trip That's Barely Started

It's been an amazing ride.

And every step of the way I've been forced to keep thinking bigger. To keep finding a bigger vision for myself.

I'm not sure where PLF goes from here. I continue to work with my PLF Owners as they launch their businesses and products in every niche and market imaginable. I've now got students who are using it in the nonprofit world. Others keep urging me to take it into the corporate world.

The one thing I know is that I would love to hear about your launch. As I said above, hearing those personal success stories never gets old.

I long ago made enough money where I could take my foot off the gas pedal and coast into semi-retirement. But here I am, somewhere around 70,000 words into this book—because I wanted to reach more people. I wanted to reach YOU.

PLF is proven. It will work for you. Just follow the steps I gave you in this book. Start building your list. Tap into the extra resources I have for you on our membership site for this book. Follow along on my blog. Plug into the PLF community.

And then write to me and tell me about your success story. You can reach me at jeff.plf@gmail.com.

Links and Resources:

Your membership site for this book: http://www.thelaunchbook.com/member

My personal blog: http://www.jeffwalker.com

Acknowledgments

The 18 years since I started my first business have been an amazing ride, and I often wonder how I got so lucky. But I didn't get here alone. I've had so many people help me on this journey that it humbles me . . .

This book is dedicated to my wife, Mary, who has always believed in and supported me so fiercely that it shocks me to this day . . . and to my two incredible children, Daniel and Joan—I don't know what I did to deserve you.

To Mom and Dad, who gave me such an incredibly loving, strong foundation for my life . . . and to Jim, Jean Marie, and Jon. I love you and thank you for who I am.

Thanks to Virginia and especially Joe Jablonsky, who believed in me when everyone else was wondering why I was home taking care of the kids. And a special thanks to Catherine Jablonsky who was an unwavering supporter in so many ways in those early uncertain years.

I've got so many other amazing people to thank . . .

Reid Tracy, Brian Kurtz, and Rick McFarland gave me great feedback on this book and helped shape the early chapters. Scott Hoffman, Brendon Burchard, Michael Hyatt, and Chris Haddad helped me with feedback on the overall book concept. Thanks to Victoria Labalme for being so darn relentless with her bigger vision of this book.

Thanks to my entire Plat Plus group who helped me brainstorm so many aspects of this book . . . and held me accountable through its long and painful birth.

This book wouldn't have been possible without my publisher Morgan James, who gracefully dealt with every curveball and missed deadline I threw at them. Thanks to David Hancock, Rick Frishman, Margo Toulouse. And a big thanks to my editor Vicki McCown, who killed dozens of my most grievous clichés before they made it to print.

So many people helped me along my path in the early days of my business, including Sheila Danzig, Mike Reed, Frank Collar, Paul Myers, and Don Cassidy.

John Reese and Yanik Silver told me I needed to start teaching people my product launch techniques, and John named PLF for me. That advice changed my life, and it changed the world.

I've had so many incredible partners, teachers, and coaches over the years—and most of them have become close friends: my coach Dan Sullivan and his wife Babs, Tony Robbins, Eben Pagan, Frank Kern, Paulo Coelho, Jeff Johnson, Rich Schefren, Ryan Deiss, Dean Graziosi, Mike Filsaime, my muse Andy Jenkins, Steven Pressfield, my DWD buddy Lisa Sasevich, Tom Kulzer, Chris Knight, Chalene and Bret Johnson, Brian Clark and Sonia Simone, Don Crowther, Marie Forleo, my study buddy Dean Jackson, Joe Polish, John Carlton, Mike Koenigs, Kenny Rueter and Travis Rosser, Jason Van Orden and Jeremy Frandsen, Chris Zavadowski, Jason Moffatt, Yaro Starak, Perry Belcher, JB Glossinger, Randy Cassingham and all the Hotshots, Audri and Jim Lanford, John Rhodes, Clay Collins, Ray Edwards, Jeff Mulligan, Ed Dale, Dave Taylor, Tim Carter, Eric Wagner, Martin Howey, Greg Poulos, Jason Potash, Pam Hendrickson, my HW community, Charles Richards, Greg Clement, Trey Smith, the FT-Talk community, Holly Lisle, Beth Walker, Shannon Waller, Anne-Marie Pratt, Denise Gosnell, Brian Sacks, Tellman Knudson, Marlon Sanders, MaryEllen Tribby, David Frey, Chris Attwood, Janet Attwood, John Jantsch, Mike Hill, Jonathan Mizel, Jay Abraham, Dan Kennedy, and Gail Kingsbury. And, of course, the Buddies (LFODMF).

Thanks to Diane Walker, who has been my amazing event planner for every live event I've done.

Can't forget my PLF Coaches, especially Alan Davidson, James Klobasa, Mark Coudray, Ridgely Goldsborough, Hubert Lee, Kurt Koenigs, Lou D'Alo . . . and especially Marc Evans—you've all helped me help my students. Thank you.

Special thanks to Ted Pasternack, who's brought his special magic to every PLF event I've ever put on. And a huge appreciation to all the "PLF Live" and Plat volunteers, including Gail, Leslie, Mel, Anthony, Michael, Jeremiah, Matt, Rebecca, Erin, Cindy, Joan, and Garrett.

And a big sanity thanks to Billy Foster, Bryan Dear, and Mac Thomson.

Another sanity check to Chris Barnes, Paul Wheeler, Rick Routh, and I'll never forget Jon Nicholas.

I wouldn't be where I'm at today, and I wouldn't be able to bring PLF to the world without my incredible team, including Marc, Mary, Shereen, Daniel, Mac, Pedro, Joy, Chereth, Larry, JR, and Paul. Special thanks to Betty Sampson, who is the true face of the company and sets the standard for customer support in the industry . . . Kristen Arnold, who is my tireless backup brain who uses her best cat-herding instincts to keep me in line. And Jon Walker, who I've been working and playing with longer than anyone.

And what can I say about my Platinum and Platinum Plus mastermind groups . . . my brothers and sisters who are in the trenches fighting the good fight with me through every epic win and seemingly insurmountable challenge. I'm blessed to have you in my life on a daily basis.

And, of course, the real stars of the show are my PLF Owners . . . who continue to inspire me every single day. Thank you.

Glossary

Please note: Some of these terms have multiple meanings and uses. This glossary gives definitions only as they're used in this book.

Affiliate Partner—a company or person who promotes another company in return for a commission on sales. Also see: Joint Venture Partner.

Call to Action—when you ask or direct your prospect to do something. This is when you ask for some type of commitment—whether it's subscribing to your list, leaving a comment, clicking a link, or buying your product. Typically, all communication you send to your list will have some type of call to action at the end of the piece.

Circle of Awesome ™—system of alternating between Seed Launch, Internal Launch, and JV Launch so that the results build on each other.

Client—someone who has already bought from you (as opposed to a Prospect, who is on your list but hasn't bought yet).

Conversion—the event where your prospect takes action based on your marketing. You've asked your prospect to take some action, and the conversion is when they commit to the action. It can refer to someone subscribing to your list, or it could be making a purchase.

Customer—see Client.

Internal Launch—a launch to your email list, where you don't have any outside JV Partners or affiliates. This is the classic PLF-style launch as described in the first eight chapters of this book.

Joint Venture Partner (or JV Partner)—almost synonymous with Affiliate Partner, although this term implies a closer working relationship with the partner.

JV Launch—a launch that is primarily driven by Affiliates and Joint Venture Partners sending traffic into your launch sequence.

Launch Conversation—the interaction between you and your prospects (as well as directly between your prospects) that naturally occurs during your Prelaunch Sequence. This interaction can give you enormous insight into your market—including the big objections to your offer and what parts of your messaging are resonating with your prospects.

Launch List—the email list you build during your Prelaunch Sequence.

Launch Sequence—your overall launch, including your Prelaunch Content and your Open Cart.

List—your database of people you'll be marketing to. Lists can be based in direct mail, social media, or email. However, in the context of this book we'll focus primarily on email lists.

List Host—a service for hosting and sending email to your email list. For recommended services, see my Resource Guide here http://thelaunchbook. com/resources.

Offer—what you're promoting to your prospects. Your offer includes your deliverables (including bonuses), your price, your payment terms, and your guarantee.

Pre-Prelaunch Sequence—also known as Pre-Pre, this is the warm-up period before your prelaunch sequence starts.

Prelaunch Sequence—a series of high-value content released before you launch to build excitement and anticipation for your product. The content can be in a variety of formats including video, PDF report, email, blog posts, etc.

Natural Search Traffic—the visitors who come to your site through your listings in the search engines. Also referred to as "organic" or "natural" traffic.

Open Cart—the time when you release your product for sale. Open Cart can refer to the actual day and time when you start taking orders and also to the entire period when your launch offer is available.

Order Page—the page where your prospects actually make their purchase. This is where they put in their contact information and payment details and click the buy button. Typically, your Sales Page will have an "Add To Cart" or "Buy It Now" button, and that button will lead to your Order Page.

Organic Search—see Natural Search Traffic.

Paid Search—paid placement at or near the top of the search engine rankings. This advertising is generally sold on a quasi-auction basis.

Paid Traffic—similar to Paid Search, except it's on non-search engine sites, such as social media sites.

PLF—Product Launch Formula®.

Prelaunch Content (or PLC)—the material you release during your Prelaunch Sequence. It can take a variety of formats including video, PDF report, email, blog posts, etc.

Product Launch Formula ® (or PLF)—pure awesomeness.

Prospect—someone who is on your list or who is looking at your marketing, but who hasn't bought yet. Once they buy, they become a Client or Customer.

Rank—where you appear in the Organic or Natural Search listings for a given search term. Can also be used in a generic global sense—e.g., "great content can help you rank in Google."

Sideways Sales Letter ™—a key component of the Product Launch Formula that refers to the serial, sequenced nature of the Prelaunch Sequence and the entire PLF sales process.

Sales Letter—a written sales message that makes the offer for a product.

Seed Launch™—a simple PLF-style launch that is primarily used if you don't have a product or a list. Can also be used if you have a concept for a new offer or product and would like to market test the idea before you spend a lot of time creating the product.

Sales Page—the web page that hosts your Sales Letter or Sales Video.

Sales Video—a video that makes the offer for a product.

Squeeze Page—a simple page on your web site that has a subscription form for your list. Visitors to the page have only one choice—they can either subscribe to your list to see more content, or they can leave the page. For recommended services for easily building squeeze pages, see my Resource Guide here http://thelaunchbook.com/resources.

Teleseminar—a conference call where the host can present to a large number of people. Everyone calls into a number and enters a PIN code to access the call. The host of the call has controls that can mute everyone while he or she presents during the call. Teleseminars can be used to teach or present material, and they're also great for making sales presentations. For recommended services for teleseminars, see my Resource Guide here http://thelaunchbook.com/resources.

Web Host—a service for hosting your web site. For recommended services, see my Resource Guide here http://thelaunchbook.com/resources.

Webinar—similar to teleseminars but presented over the web so attendees can see the presenter's computer screen. Most often used to display a Powerpoint or Keynote presentation. For recommended services for webinars, see my Resource Guide here http://thelaunchbook.com/resources.

About the Author

Jeff Walker has literally transformed the way stuff is sold online. Along the way he's become one of the top entrepreneurial and marketing trainers in the world.

Back in the old days before he started teaching his "Product Launch Formula", almost no one in the online entrepreneurial world talked about "product launches" and the idea of a "million dollar day" seemed almost ludicrous. But now, in the post-Product Launch Formula world, the million dollar (and multi-million dollar) launches hardly raise an eyebrow. They've almost become routine.

But his techniques are not just for big gurus—he's taught thousands of students (who operate in hundreds of niches), and they've generated more than $500 million in sales (and that number grows every day.)

Jeff lives in Durango, Colorado where he pursues his passions for all kinds of outdoor fun. He lives with his wife Mary and their dog Jenny. And even though the children are out of the house, Jeff still has lots of adventures with them (especially on skis and mountain bikes).

You can follow Jeff on his blog at JeffWalker.com, and get free training on marketing and launches at ProductLaunchFormula.com.